THIS BOOK IS FOR YOU IF...

- You suffer daily stressful events
- You want to know why things become stressful
- You need a coping strategy to deal with the burden of daily life
- You desire a more peaceful and relaxed life
- You have too many idiots around you
- You need an easy way to understand what makes them so stupid
- You have a need to stop shouting at them
- You want to know how to handle these people and have an easier life
- You urgently need to change something in your life
- You know your need for change is strong but you are going to fail (again)
- You want to learn how to direct your efforts so you can conquer change
- You want a better life for yourself

You need this book if you want less stress in your life and want to live in a better world. We only have one life; why make it a stressful one? Why not enjoy it?

Carl

"Carl Rosier-Jones helps us to identify our personal stresses and picture them as woolly Mammoths, then teaching us how our personality type can make our Mammoths extinct and thus combat stress effectively. As a sufferer of Post Traumatic Stress Disorder myself, the book resonates strongly with me. I am slowly learning to rid myself of my Mammoths!"

Jenny Hawkins

"I couldn't put the book down. What I liked is how the author explains how we can get stressed at the least little thing and how to help to control it. I found it an eye-opener for me and it has made me think of how to make my life less stressful by just dealing with things in a calm way. I would recommend anyone who suffers with stress or know someone that does to buy it. Will read it again."

Tina Chissell

"I bought this book after hearing of the author's real-life brush with death and wondered if his experience had resulted in a new perspective on stress. What I found was an easy to relate to and easy to read, funny and thought-provoking book; all in a 'that sounds uncannily like my friend' sort of way. He uses easy language and engaging stories to bring the characters to life and help make stress less of a thing to be feared but, rather, understood and exploited by helping us all understand our own triggers and coping strategies that little bit better."

Stuart Coffey

WHERE DID ALL THIS STRESS COME FROM?

Many years ago, our Caveman ancestors developed a survival technique. It was designed to keep them alive. They would push their button when they needed it.

The button is a tiny gland that sits on top of their kidneys. When they needed something extra when threatened, a press of their button (the 'adrenal medulla gland') produced an adrenaline discharge that pumped straight into their bloodstream, priming their muscles to either fight or flight. The fight or flight button helped our Caveman ancestors in many different ways, making them more reactive, stronger, allowing clearer thinking and, when needed, giving them super human strength.

If our Caveman ancestors came face to face with a Mammoth, a push of their button gave them what they needed.

A few million years later, we still have our life-saving button, but with no Mammoths around, why do we still need it?

Do not be shocked, but Mammoths are not extinct!

Yes, Mammoths are still here; they would win the National Hide and Seek Championships if they were to enter. Mammoths are sneaky and underhanded. They have mastered the art of hiding in plain sight, in normal everyday situations. They are camouflaged in traffic jams, cover themselves up using emails, and squeeze themselves into the smallest of places.

When the time is right, modern-day Mammoths pounce! They only show themselves for a fraction of a second and only to their intended victim; it is just long enough to make us want to push our button!

The Caveman Stress Principles will help people understand and control their buttons. It will benefit individuals and teams of people who want to reduce stress and gain control of their stress.

ABOUT THE AUTHOR

Carl Rosier-Jones is a Stress Coach and a Stress Consultant. Having worked in a particularly stressful environment himself, he observed at first-hand the devastating effects that stress has on people, himself included. Reducing stress became his passion, and can even be described as an obsession by those who are close to him! His research into the subject helped him to create his Caveman Principles.

The writing and publishing of this book has given him a greater reach and a platform to help many more people cope with their daily stressful struggle.

Carl runs Caveman Principles Training Workshops, where he delivers his theories, and uses metaphors to help support and discuss his delegates' stress events, with the aim to leave them with a new understanding of stress. He is passionate about wanting to work with people who need his help, as he believes the Caveman Principles is the new and proven technique for helping them conquer stress.

DEDICATION

My thanks go to my wife, Karen and my son, Harrison, mainly because they have had to put up with me.

I try not to let them know that they are being used as my guinea pigs, but I am discovered more often than not, so now I am putting up my hands and coming clean about all this.

My thanks go to my employer and to all the amazing friends and colleagues I have met there. Most have had to work with me in a 'pressure cooker' of a day job, which has been the biggest proving ground for the content of this book.

The Caveman Tribe, including all the Mammoths, were drawn by a talented young artist, Scott Theobald. Thank you, Scott, for your hard work and your dedication; we got there and we have made the tribe memorable.

Thank you to my clients, who have listened to my talks, followed my advice and gave me fantastic feedback. All of it has helped me gather my thoughts and create this book.

Without all these people, I would never have written this book, and it would never have been such a personal success.

GET RID OF EVERYDAY STRESS WITH THE CAVEMAN PRINCIPLES AND ENJOY MAMMOTH SUCCESS

CARL ROSIER-JONES

Published in the United Kingdom by
Filament Publishing Ltd
16 Croydon Road,
Waddon, Croydon
Surrey, CR0 4PA

www.filamentpublishing.com
+44(0)20 8688 2598

The Caveman Principles by Carl Rosier-Jones
ISBN 978-1-910819-39-5
© 2015 Carl Rosier-Jones

Printed by IngramSpark

TABLE OF CONTENTS

IT'S NOT STRESS
THAT KILLS US.
IT IS OUR REACTION
TO IT.

HANS SELYE

WHERE DO WE START?

The origins of the stressed caveman, followed by 'The Caveman Principles'.

What has this book got to do with palaeoanthropology? The short answer is 'not one tiny bit'. But it has everything to do with stress, communication and change, especially for the modern Caveman.

Academics are going to hate this book. Luckily, it was not written for them, it was written for you, the modern Caveman. Explanations within this book do not get too deep; it was written with enough information and examples to help you pick up the useful tools for everyday life, mixed up with a smidgen of humour.

If you are of the female persuasion, don't let the title put you off. 'Caveman' has been used as the generic term for a very, very long time. It is the old ancestor of ours and the term covers both sexes. This book is not necessarily for just 'him indoors'; it was written for all modern Cavepeople.

It has been written by a bloke, with little female influence, but it has been written for everyone to enjoy.

Warning: there is not going to be a 'big dig' in this book and there is not even going to be a snippet of a time machine. There will be no complex mathematics for you to have to worry about and no final exam. Although there will be some anthropology (the study of human behaviour), it will be buried within the pages of this book, and I promise it will be painless.

I also promise that it has been written by someone who understands soulless books and it has been designed to be an enjoyable read. I hope it changes you from a novice to an expert in understanding the Caveman Principles and most importantly, I hope you find this book a fun and interesting read.

I invite anyone with a slight interest of finding out how humans think to have a dig around in this book. If it piques your interest and you want to visit a real Caveman Tribe, then either come and see my family, or if that is too dangerous, you're going to have to figure out that time machine thing by yourself.

Now I have set the tone for this book, a simple, straightforward and only slightly humorous read, I hope you enjoy it. As with any book, I have a website for those who want more information and want to sign up to my newsletter: www.carlrosierjones.com

Before we start this journey and get into the tasty stuff, can I tell you the reason why I wrote this book? If you're not interested flick to chapter one, otherwise I promise this is the only place you will get my 'heartfelt' story, so if you're still with me, let's get it over with.

You see, all my life, all I wanted to do was wear a hat. I didn't know why or even what one I wanted to wear. I suppose wearing a hat gave me a purpose and an identity. When I got my first proper hat, I wanted to wear loads more. I wanted to collect them, as many as I could.

My first hat came when I joined Wiltshire Police. After I completed my training, I was allowed to wear lots more hats as I trained in different roles. All these extra hats came with additional responsibilities, but it meant I could add to my head-covering collection.

Then the police ran out of hats that I could collect. I had collected all the ones I had wanted, so where could I go to get more opportunities to get and wear extra ones?

There could have been roles in the police where I could train and have new skills, but if it didn't come with a new hat, I could not really see the point.

So I looked outside the police and found the Royal Air Force, joining as a reserve. Some may think that was a bit extreme just to get a few new hats, but I can honestly say that I enjoyed wearing every single hat that the RAF wanted to give to me. From my beret to my Kevlar helmet, not forgetting my 'number 1' cap.

I wore all my hats with pride and when I did, I felt that I was part of something, that when I put one of them on, I felt different, honoured and complete.

Both organisations gave me plenty of opportunity to wear as many of my hats as I possibly could. Some of my hats were designed to stop my head from being kicked in or to have a sudden injection of lead, but I still enjoyed wearing those 'danger' hats.

I was juggling about 12 to 15 different hats in total, and many people thought that I was crazy for doing so. They'd say to me, "Are you crazy?"

I just carried on wearing the hats, doing my two jobs and I found a fulfilment in my life like no other. With hindsight, none of these hats caused me any stress, even when I wore them in times that others would not even be able to dream of.

I felt no stress whilst in the middle of a 'bring your own bricks' riot or in the 'heat' of the Afghanistan desert during the summer months. These hats were an identity; I trusted them and I cherished being part of something that I considered to be worthwhile.

My family and friends were telling me that I was burning the candle at both ends. They put doubt in my mind. They would try telling me that I had no downtime, no time for myself and my constant 'on the go' lifestyle could not be good for me.

I carried on regardless, ignoring the negative vibes being sent my way, until I had to make a choice. My full-time job, the police, made it impossible for me to train at weekends with the Air Force after they changed the shift pattern and took away all the flexibility. I had no option but to hang up my beret and walk away from the Air Force. I almost cried when I handed in my early termination notice.

Then I started to become ill. I was not sleeping, not feeling myself and felt that I was no longer enjoying life. It turned into a real slog just to get up in the morning and do what I thought I enjoyed doing, being a Police Officer. I was still putting on a hat but a big chunk of me felt like it was missing. My nature has always been to fix things, to find out why things happen. Many hours of soul searching, reading and counselling sessions passed before I discovered it. It took years of my time before I came to my own conclusion. For me, my jobs were my interests and they were not the problem. I had been looking in the wrong place. When I found the source of my illness, it was not a great surprise. It was stress.

Wearing all those hats was not the reason for this stress. The hats were an outlet that I believed was my joy to wear and my choice to do so.

Wearing some of my hats made me LOSE part of my identity. Had it of been my decision to quit the Air Force, I would have accepted it, but it was the change of shift pattern at my work that was being forced upon me. This 'change' was the start of my stress.

As I was being forced to adjust to this change, I noticed my interactions with people were getting harder. Those who I thought were supposed to be there to support and help me, seemed to be ignoring me and they felt distant. The people at work were not who I thought they were, and my friends seemed to change overnight.

It was my chance to look at and analyse human interactions. I had to try new methods of communication and form new friendships.

My interest in 'people watching' paid off. Not in a creepy, illegal way; I just found it fascinating to watch how people interacted with each other. How quickly things can change when people became stressed, friendships are broken and new alliances made. What these people did and, more interestingly, what they thought they were doing, was fascinating to me. I had discovered a new interest and a new outlet, but it didn't come with a hat, so I made one.

I found most people are not very comfortable being forthright, asking for what they want. Then throw in some stress, especially in a work environment, and watch what happens. They all act and react differently, or so I thought. I realised there was something to all these interactions, and ended up researching human psychology. Myers Briggs was my first stop, along with William Marston, which led me to researching the origins of categorising people. I found Hippocrates (the greatest Greek Physician c.460-c.370 BC) had used 'four humours,' which reflects in some of today's modern theories. Categorising personalities has been around for over 2,000 years and I had just discovered it, but it was confusing.

With a new interest and a thirst to understand it, I started to shove people into my own boxes. These boxes started to fill up and were showing unique character traits. My theories were being formed from my boxes.

I wanted to make my own modern-day, helpful, profiling list that I could use. I worked out who and what was in each box, all the common traits were written down, and then I had enough information to help me identify these categories of people.

I wanted to be able to identify each new personality, putting them into a box within minutes of meeting them. I never asked their permission, so they had no idea what I was doing. I found my character trait theory was working, and it was getting me results.

At work, I spoke to victims and offenders of crime, colleagues and managers, friends and family; all of these people I began to see in a different light as I started to shove them into the boxes I had prepared. Some of these people I began to like more as I started to understand how they worked and operated. With this new insight, I thought I had just won the lottery. I was able to categorise people and work out the best way to speak to them and how to manage them.

I have used my new box technique to communicate better, to understand what has been happening around me, and I have found new friends that once I thought I would never like. I can work people out faster, learn their true thoughts and feelings long before they feel the need to say them. I can anticipate their wants and needs, which has made me become a better person, and ultimately a better Police Officer.

Using the information I gathered from my people watching and box stuffing exercises, having interviewed unsuspecting individuals and reading even more books on this subject, I was able to produce what I needed, a usable 'people' system.

It had been fun and exciting to work all this out. I still wear my new hat; perhaps one day I will show it to you, but until then, I will continue to use and refine my new theory as there is always something new and exciting to discover.

I also felt I needed to work out other things that were bothering me. I found my understanding of stress and change management was lacking greatly. My research and new understanding in these subjects made me appreciate how complex these areas can be. I thought that people needed to be aware of these things, but understood that when things are too complicated, people become distracted. I wanted to find a new way to use all this information, and wanted to do it by making it fun and interesting. Then I found a gem. All my research just came together and I found what I had been looking for. My theories fitted perfectly with my new people profiling system; it all worked.

Putting it all together, I found I had an answer to how I could manage my stress, the Caveman Principles.

I practiced my theories on my friends, family and then on complete strangers I found propping up the bar whilst on holiday. I would let them into my secret of personality profiling, stress and change management. I became a bit of an expert on the subject, and felt a little like a celebrity as I was introduced to others as the Caveman bloke. For the entire 10 minutes I was allowed to talk about my theory, I felt great, then my wife would get bored and take me away from my adoring crowd, or was it just away from the bar?

It was a brilliant ice-breaker, and many people I have spoken to in the bar have become lifelong friends. Just from these short interactions, it kept popping up in the conversations, keeping them alive for the entire length of our holiday. We all swapped emails before we left for home, and I never thought anything more about it.

Then during the 2014 Christmas period, out of the blue I was contacted by email from one of these 'holiday bar' people. I met her on a cruise. She must have gone through her bin to find my email address. Her name was Becks and she was from Australia.

I could remember Becks. I thought she was easily impressed with my theories, so I enjoyed going over the same theories again and again with her, thinking it was all a bit of harmless fun. She asked if I could write down some of my thoughts for her so she could have a proper read later, which I did and thought nothing more about them. We would all chat for hours at the bar each night, profiling other guests and even the staff. It was just a laugh, or so I told myself.

Coming back to Becks' email, she told me that when she got back home from holiday, she started to use my theories. She went back to work, used her new profiling skills, and she found a wonderful new way to interact with her boss. She said she had gotten herself promoted within months of her using my system, something she said she had not been able to do for many years before we had met. She said it was all because of my stress and communication system that I had taught her in the bar.

This was my wake-up call. I had a system that I could teach people, even when the classroom was a bar and I was a bit tipsy.

All I needed was a delivery method, to make a sensitive, uninteresting subject more fun and accessible to others. I decided on delivering talks to interested groups and writing this book.

We all live busy, stressful lives, but we possess the ability to shape and mould our future. The only person who holds 'us' back, is you. We can blame others, our boss, our wife/ husband or even the kids, but ultimately you are the only person who can change your life.

I developed the Caveman Principles to make my life better and I know that now I have shared it, it will help you as well. The book has been written to put these theories in an easy to read guide. You can follow them and improve your own life. You have the power to make the choice, to want better relationships, manage change easily and, more importantly, reduce your own stress. I hope you embrace the Caveman Principles and find them useful.

USING THIS BOOK

This book has been written to give you what you want (what we all want) – an easier and better life!

This book has been written for you. You should be scribbling in the margins and folding corners of pages as you go. For those who do not like to ruin books, you can download some of the exercises from my website: www.carlrosierjones.com. Both the book and the website have been put together to help you understand and reduce your personal stress, to give you a system that will assist you in understanding people better, and provide you with a process to help you cope with and accept change in your life.

If you want to read this book from cover to cover, please feel free and start on page one.

If you wish to use this book as a dip in and out, 'as' and 'when' needed type of reference book, then I have divided it into three parts;

If you:
- have trouble sleeping
- difficulty in switching off
- find you are always ill with coughs and colds
- feel wound up to the point of exploding
- know you need some form of release
- need to know how not get so stressed

...then you need to dive straight into Part 1. Here you will find a simple explanation and a method of how to identify stress. What you need to know about the good and the bad stuff.

If you want:
- a better relationship (at work, home or social)
- to have better rapport with people
- to know how to deal with difficult people
- better interactions with others
- to know why you express yourself in certain ways
- to get an understanding of why people act oddly

...then skip over to Part 2. This is where you will find out which part of the tribe you belong to. Then you can read how to identify the other tribe members and how you can interact and communicate with them better.

If you:
- are going through a challenging time (work or home)
- want to do something different
- have a personal goal you want to stick to (this time)
- have to make some adjustments in your life
- are feeling a resistance of doing something unfamiliar
- need to understand what change really means

...then the last section of this book is for you. Change is never nice, but if you can talk to your inner caveman and learn how to steer his pet Mammoth, resistance can be a thing of the past. Learn how to turn change from a negative word to a positive one.

Ultimately it does not matter if you want to read this whole book or dip in and out. You can also leave it on a shelf collecting dust, but it is here and it will help you.

You are the only one who has the power to make a difference in your life. I took the challenge of writing this book and I feel proud to have put so much effort into it, but to start it I had to make the choice, and that was that I had to do; 'something'. You only have one life (unless you are a practicing Buddhist monk), so make it memorable.

After reading this book, you will start your journey, you will need some helpful advice or some refresher training, so keep this book close to hand so you can swot up or check my website for the next training dates.

You do not need to know the content of this book off by heart but if you do, please get in touch and perhaps if I get enough replies, I can run a Caveman Competition.

Please enjoy the book, stay faithful to your tribe and please do not operate heavy machinery whilst reading it.

If you feel the need to get in contact with me, for whatever reason, don't be a stranger, drop me an email. I would love to hear from you. If you want to share how *The Caveman Principles* have helped you, then let me know. The best stories will find their way on to my web page; don't worry, I can change names to protect the innocent.

I genuinely hope you find the contents useful and as fulfilling as I have found writing them.

Just think 'Caveman' style.
www.carlrosierjones.com

"I don't have any yet. We just opened."

THE GREATEST WEAPON
AGAINST STRESS
IS OUR ABILITY
TO CHOOSE ONE THOUGHT
OVER ANOTHER.

WILLIAM JAMES

PART ONE

I. THE ORIGINS OF STRESS

Have you heard, there is Good and Bad Stress?

"It's called 'stress' — It'll help with natural selection."

Stress is a daily human response, nothing more and nothing less, regardless of what others may tell you. Complications come when we forget this fact and we end up making 'things' far too complicated, all in an attempt to be less stressed.

It is our body's natural reaction to an unexpected event or during a challenging time when stress kicks in. Stress is something that most people believe they know everything there is to know about it but they have very little control over this reaction. This part of the book will give an understanding, one you may not have been aware of, and with this new knowledge, you will begin to gain control.

We have all had our fair share of the nasty stuff, but what is stress, where does it come from, and what does it do to us? Some people know how stress affects them and may be able to sense when stress is building up. They seem to do something about it before it is too late (we may hate these 'Zen' masters). You know the ones, they always have some 'hippy' comment to make, whereas we'd rather throw a chair at someone's head and hand in our resignation, probably written in blood (preferably someone else's blood).

This part of the book will help you understand stress and in time and with practice, you will be able to control it.

The reason you are reading this is probably because you want to deal with stress. You are probably stressed right now; this is the bad stuff and you need help with it.

Stress is caused every week, every day, every hour and every minute, but we are not aware of it. The biggest problem about stress is that we no longer understand what it was designed to do and we no longer give it the respect it really deserves. The effects of bad stress should never be underestimated. It can cause illness, break friendships, ruin marriages and cause mental health issues to the unfortunate few.

Bad stress is more real; it has more impact in our lives than anyone would care to admit. Stress cannot be seen, held, touched, measured or even predicted by others, and although people say they are 'stressed', no one will know what the full impact means, not even the sufferer. Most will not even know that they are stressed and will not even be aware of their reactions, until it is too late. People do not know how this stress reaction was caused and, more importantly, will not be interested in wanting to know. They may just apologise and want to move on, seeing it as a weakness rather than a learning opportunity.

Stress reactions can be traced to one specific incident but most people will not know why it triggered the reaction. They may have done the same task a hundred times before and on that one occasion, it caused them to boil over. These reactions probably have happened many times before but as it has only been papered over and not addressed, the next time it happens it will be worse, and that time it may cause them to want to start tearing the place apart and anyone else who gets in their way.

Let's start by explaining the stress response. Don't worry, there is not going to be a biology lesson here, no talk of blood or guts, and no dissection of any wee beasties either. Biology 101, pure and simple, stress is a word used to describe our body telling us that we are under threat of an imminent attack. Our body has a hardwired system to deal with threats and is something that our bodies have a natural reaction against; it is a survival instinct.

When potentially normal situations catch us unaware, it causes panic and the stress reflex automatically kicks in.

For example, have you ever been speaking to someone, been so engrossed in the conversation, that when a friend walks up to your side and says hello, it sets off an uncontrolled reaction. You've been 'spooked'! You found yourself six feet in the air or in a full sprint running for the hills. Can you remember anything between being scared half to death and then coming back to your senses?

You were probably clutching your chest, catching your breath before you realised you were not in danger, but what danger? What made you react like this?

I bet you had no idea why you got to that stage; you just laughed it off and never gave it a second thought.

How about a more serious situation? Have you ever been thrown into a life or death scenario, finding extraordinary strength to do something really brave? Have you ever saved your own life, or that of another? Maybe you were crossing a road and never seeing that car come racing towards you? Somehow, before you knew it, you were stood on the pavement completely unharmed and the car just drives past.

How did you get from the middle of the road to the safety of the path in a split second? Imagine doing this with your child holding your hand. You look down and see that they are unharmed, smiling up at you; how did you get yourself and your little one to safety so fast?

If you have ever been in a situation or even in a tighter squeeze than running across a road, did you notice that your body just took over? Can you honestly say that you were in control of any of your thoughts or actions? This is the stress button working at its best.

There are some extreme cases of people using their stress reflex getting reported in the news or even posted on YouTube videos. You know, the ones that get shared a million times on Facebook, as people watch in astonishment and ask if it is real. Documented examples are shared around the entire world within seconds and are always popping up on someone's newsfeed. These extraordinary feats only happen because people push their stress button.

These drastic responses have been given a name of 'hysterical strength'. Examples include mothers lifting cars off their children who are trapped underneath, people jumping from one building to the next to get away from a fire, and even adults fighting fully grown polar bears to save children from being eaten.

Whether you were just spooked or you need to find the strength and courage to fight a polar bear, it all comes from the same place, the stress button.

Stress buttons are pushed when we need the 'fight or flight' response. Everyone has probably heard of this phrase but how many know of its origins? The expression regularly pops up in conversation, when people talk about scary experiences. Some people may know of its origins and a few more may know the effect it has on the human body.

Knowing where it comes from and what it does to the body is the start of getting to grips with the bad stuff.

First, we need to get the word 'stress' out of the naughty bin; not all stress is bad. There is good stuff as well. You will just have read that stress is needed to lift a car off someone or required to jump large distances to save your life. These extreme reactions are all stress-related and should not be seen as being bad. It is just our body doing what it was designed to do.

There are more of the everyday 'good' stresses that need to be mentioned in this book. What about using stress when we need a little extra focus or concentration? In an exam, we may need some clearer thoughts, or in a race a little extra strength. The extra boost that a button push can give can mean the difference between a pass and a fail, or first and second place.

Good stress, or the Eustress response, allows people to reach new or higher goals. It is used best when we want something which is just out of our reach. When we push for a goal, we place extra stress on ourselves, creating a managed but stressful situation which triggers the push of the button (think of the film *The Dark Knight Rises* when Batman wants out of 'the pit').

When we achieve better results, we put it down to the hard work and dedication. There is little recognition that a push of the stress button helped out.

Then we have the bad stuff, the reason why this book was written. This is the stuff of nightmares. This negative stress is why so many people need help. Bad stress is why we overeat, shout, lose it, use alcohol, or just want to curl up somewhere and be left alone. It's horrible because if it takes hold of people, it is almost impossible to shake it off, without asking for help.

How can one of our body's major life-saving reactions make us superheroes one moment, and the next make us the most unpleasant person on the planet?

Over the course of human history, natural body reaction has put great leaders in front of us, and it is also responsible for leaving others in the deepest, darkest crevices of their human psyches.

Bad stress was the reason I wanted to write this book. Part of writing any book is the research and the forming of opinions along with conclusions. I thought it would help you to start on the good stuff, then move into the bad.

It is only the bad stress that gets recognition. It causes all of us problems, so never feel alone. It comes from all sorts of places, like changes in our lifestyles, having to deal with irritating people, and work pressure.

When people experience the bad stuff, they do not know how to handle it. When people hear someone is struggling with the bad stuff, they also don't know how to handle it. Without guidance, people make matters worse and create massive problems for themselves and others.

It is normally handled by so-called friends telling people to 'man up, buttercup'. This response is normally after an announcement made on a Facebook posting of "Not happy..." which is followed by about 100 responses of "What's up, hun?" or the one I like to use, "Which one are you then?"

If the source of the stress is ignored, it allows people to wallow in self-pity. The impact that this prolonged stressful situation is having on our bodies is immeasurable. The mishandling of bad stress causes a perfectly natural bodily reaction, to manifest into pain and illness.

The answer to all of this is to get back in control of this reaction. To understand stress, stop thinking of it as all bad, treat it with respect and, most importantly, start to handle it better.

The best place to start is the origins of stress, the basic human nature 'fight or flight' reaction.

This reaction contributes a lot more to our everyday life than most people think. It is the starting place to understand stress. Before we move on, the first hurdle is to ask that people think of stress as a whole and not just the bad stuff. It's time we dragged it out of the naughty corner.

ADOPTING THE RIGHT ATTITUDE CAN CONVERT A NEGATIVE STRESS INTO A POSITIVE ONE.

HANS SELYE

2. FIGHT OR FLIGHT

How do Cavemen become stressed?

Stress comes from the 'fight or flight' response which I mentioned in the last chapter. Understanding the fight or flight reaction is easy; however, I need to take you back a few million years.

I know I promised there were no time machines, so you'll just have to use your imagination. Go back to when we were just starting to walk on two feet. Think about how we managed to find new ways to wear a loincloth as well (to save any embarrassment or excitement).

We lived together in tribes and we were the main meals for many bigger, stronger animals.

We had natural animal pack instincts. We would live together and hunt together in packs that made us strong. The tribe was not easily attacked by other animals and we were able to live in relative safety.

Tribes made us strong as we could fend off attacks from these bigger, more dangerous animals. We could protect and feed our young, and care for the injured at the same time. We would ensure that our other tribe members were fit and healthy, that we all had enough food so that everyone was fed and comfortable.

The early Caveman had help with these things; he had developed a button. I know, I promised there would be no Biology lesson but this next bit is important, so let me explain.

The 'button' is a tiny gland that sits on top of our kidneys. When the brain thought it was being threatened or in a dangerous situation, it had the capability to push that button. When the button is pressed, it helped the body do some truly wonderful and unexpected things.

Let's see the button working in our new Caveman friend; let's call him Bert. Bert is a ferocious and brilliant Hunter, and he always brings home the meat for his tribe. Bert leaves the cave in a Hunter pack. They all carry their weapons and they spend days hunting their prey. They laugh and joke as they work, and are feeling quite relaxed roaming the land.

They start to track a Woolly Mammoth. These are bigger than today's modern elephants, and much more dangerous. By himself, Bert knows that he does not stand a chance, but as a pack, they have every chance of bringing home enough meat to feed his entire tribe for weeks.

Up until now, Bert has been enjoying the company of his fellow Hunters, and his only thoughts have been to concentrate on finding his next meal. Then he finds the Mammoth and his attitude changes. Bert sneaks up closer to it. As he gets closer to the Mammoth, he suddenly starts to feel different. There are some short-term changes going on in his body. He feels an excited fizz growing; his focus has pinpointed on the Mammoth. These feelings are growing stronger as he starts to get closer to his prey.

To help Bert transform from an everyday carefree Caveman to a hardened Hunter becoming totally focused on the job in hand, he has developed the button.

There is experience and training involved, but the use of his stress button plays an important part. A press of his button will give him extra focus, extra strength, and now he is ready to kill the Mammoth.

His body needs to be ready. His mind has to be cleared of everything but the Mammoth. He has to be alert, watching and waiting for the unknown, being able to respond within a second's notice at whatever comes his way.

Bert's brain has recognised a 'kill or be killed' scenario. It is being threatened with danger; even though it is Bert's conscious decision to be there, it still pushes the stress button. That tiny little gland sat on his kidneys injects adrenaline into Bert's body.

This makes his muscles and limbs come alive and ready for action. The push of the button also pumps lots of other nasty toxins into his body, all of them designed to make his reasoning and reactions razor-sharp. These different toxins start a chemical reaction, focusing his mind, clearing his body of unwanted waste and doing odd things like making his skin extra sensitive and his hearing become selective. His heart rate rises, pumping blood around his body into his limbs, ready to feed his muscles when the time is needed. Bert's eyes have widened so he can now see the smallest of movement in the finest of detail; all thoughts of his family, his 'to-do' list and how he looks in his new loincloth have been purged from his mind.

Bert is ready for the fight. A push of the stress button has turned him into a single-minded, focused, superstrong, killing machine. Bert is not alone; all the other Hunters in the pack will have also pushed their buttons, and all of them are ready to strike.

They run at superfast speeds, are able to jump higher, swing harder and react quicker. They are able to work harder and overpower the Mammoth because of their stress button. When the dust settles, all of the Hunters are exhausted. It is the end of the fight, but they have achieved their goal.

The push of their buttons delivered all the adrenaline that they needed; it helped them win the fight but now it has been burnt off through fierce exercise, along with those nasty toxins that were used to focus the mind. They return to their normal carefree Caveman-style, and those temporary superpowers have gone.

They will be exhausted, but they have their prize and their entire tribe can eat. They drag what they can back to the cave feeling proud of themselves and of their achievement. They are exhausted and they know they need rest before their next hunt.

The fight or flight button has other uses, other than when it is needed for hunting. Bert's brother, Errol, likes to wander off from the cave by himself. He enjoys collecting berries and other useful items, like sticks (ready for when the tribe invents fire).

Now Errol is happy pushing his way through the bushes and undergrowth, picking the ripest of berries and thinking of nothing in particular other than the warm sunshine on his back. Suddenly, he pulls back a branch and he comes face to face with a Mammoth. He has no spear and no team of Hunters around him; his brain know that his life is in danger and he knows it.

Errol's brain immediately recognises the threat and it pushes the fight or flight button, just like Bert had done when he had faced his Mammoth. The difference is that this Mammoth was unexpected and Errol did not have the chance to prepare himself.

Errol's body reacts the same as Bert's had done. An injection of adrenaline was squirted into his system and all those toxins pumped into his organs making him strong and agile. His mind is clear and its focus is on survival. His ability to react has sped up, his brain speed has increased. He can instantly see an escape route. His entire body is in a heightened state of readiness.

Without needing to think for himself, Errol is already on his toes. He has automatically dropped everything that is going to slow him down and he is already at full speed, sprinting from the threat of the Mammoth before it has a chance to think about doing anything to hurt him.

Errol is able to run all the way back to the cave and when he gets there, he is exhausted but elated that he is still alive. His running has exercised his body, burning away all those toxins and adrenaline that had been squirted into his system. He needs time to recover and takes the rest of the day off before he goes back out looking for food and sticks. As Errol sprinted away from the danger, just like Bert fighting with his Mammoth, both their bodies used up everything that was provided by the push of their stress buttons. They both live to see another day and they know the risks they face the next time they go out. They take the time they need to recover properly and then are set to do it all again.

The fight or flight button is a life-saving tool. It ensured Bert and Errol, our Caveman ancestors, were able to survive in the tough world they knew back then. These smart, stress button-pushing Cavemen developed into today's homo sapiens.

We may be taller, less hairy and have better teeth but most of our internal organs, gizmos and thingamabobs are the same, including the 'fight or flight' button.

3. LOOK OUT FOR MODERN-DAY MAMMOTHS

Modern-day Cavemen.

Just like our ancestors, we were not built for modern-day society. Over the last 50 years, people have found new ways to live, socialise, work, travel and play, but our bodies have not had a chance to evolve that quickly. If we could ask for changes in evolution, we could do with a USB socket located somewhere and to get rid of the unsightly back hair most men have... and what is the appendix used for?

In today's world, most of us live in a negative, fear-driven, and even a numb feeling environment. This type of lifestyle gets harder every day; it gets harder to smile and to start feeling things again.

We all live busy, hectic lifestyles, and we plan fun things for the weekends or for our holidays, but end up using this time for sleeping or recovering, ready to restart on Monday morning.

We all know what life should be like but we don't stop to question the treadmill existence we find ourselves in. We just get on with it, mainly because we do not know an alternative. We accept that this is society and if we want to become part of it, we have to put up with it. These negative emotions become part of that lifestyle. Bad events happen to us and we accept that this is 'life'.

This may sound a little melodramatic and a 'woe is me' type tale but it does have a point to make. I expect most people reading this feel this way sometimes, if not sometimes then probably all the time. This is a sign that bad stress has crept into our lives and it is making us suffer like this.

We are probably not aware that this constant negativity is there and that it is a really bad environment to live in. We can be so 'materialist' and 'driven' that we believe we have to live like this, only so we can have nice things. We become numb to the fact that there should be joy and freedom in everything that we do.

Instead we have come to accept that if we want nice things, people are allowed to treat us badly and what is worse, we can do the same to others. What a nasty and vicious cycle modern Cavemen have gotten themselves into.

Wow, that got even heavier! Sorry if it came out strongly there but sometimes a slap around the face with a wet fish is better than being sat on the beach enjoying the view, not seeing the tidal wave coming right at you.

I wanted to make this book an easy read but what would be the point if it didn't have an impact on you, especially if it is here to help. Those last few paragraphs were written to make you sit up and take stock. You see, we are all letting our lives drift by (me included), and only when someone points something out do we realise what has been going on. So to make the point, let me show you how negative we have become.

It's a good job I will only do this in this chapter; the rest of the book is all positive stuff. Just get through this next bit. At least there isn't going to be any of that complicated maths stuff which normally goes with these types of books.

Let me show you how negative society has become. How many ways do we have to describe human emotions using the English language?

You can leave the Oxford dictionary on the shelf (or in the box in the garage): there are roughly 560 different words to tell someone how we are feeling. Being that I am a bloke, that means there are 560 different ways for me to say, "I'm OK."

For a female, that is 560 different ways they can tell a bloke that things are not "OK."

My wife thinks I have the emotional range of a wet sock. To me, being called a damp piece of material covering a foot is not so bad in the grand scheme of 'emotional' things.

For my female readers, a small insight into a bloke's mind. Again, I can only speak as a bloke, but I believe things are normally good or bad. Blokes are either happy or 'busy'. This pretty much sets out the range of emotions that most men will normally want to share.

Now get ready for the real surprise. Out of those 560 emotions, 345 of them describe a negative emotion such as sadness, sorrow and upset. The mathematicians reading this may have just worked out that there must be only 215 to describe the good ones, like being happy, joyed and satisfied. I did not separate the neutral emotions, such as OK, from the positive emotions, because as stated above, this is a normal bloke response to things being good.

If you want to use a calculator, or if you trust my maths, 62% of our emotional descriptive words describe our negative emotions. There are almost twice as many ways to express the bad emotions in our lives, than we have to use for the positive ones.

We only have 38% of the emotional words in the dictionary that we can use to describe the good feelings and emotions that we should be having every day. No wonder we live in a negative state when it is easier to find a negative emotion than a good one.

Another example of how negative our society has become is to count how many soap operas there are on television and how popular they are by looking at the viewing figures. They seem to be the nation's favourite daily addiction. People need their serialised drama input, with the soap writers competing against each other to make the next storyline the 'worst' possible. People love to watch constant cliffhangers and to see others act out their pain. It doesn't stop there as people then relive it at work, gossiping about the last episode and guessing at the future plot lines.

Soaps are on almost every national television channel. Society cannot seem to get enough of them. The sheer number of different soaps is rising, as well as the frequency of the number of shows per week. The length of episodes keep getting extended and they all get repeated so people can catch up.

People enjoy the suspense of a 'good' soap drama but what they are doing is something that is very bad for their emotions.

They are living these traumas themselves. They become embroiled in the anger, fury, upset and despair that the actors portray on the screen.

One more fact to indicate that society likes to live in a negative state is the constant need for news. It can be watched anytime and anywhere because there is a demand. There are loads of 24-hour news stations, phone apps, newspapers and, of course, the 'news chat' around the kettle at work. All report on national and international news stories, most of them have no bearing or impact on us. Yet we want to sit and watch updates on terrible news stories that are happening on the other side of the world. All of this negative input is designed to do one thing, sell news; it is big business. The news agencies understand society's need and want to hear and see these things, so they find news stories anywhere they can to feed people's appetites.

Bringing this chapter back to modern-day stress, you can see that being in a negative society can be unhealthy. It is not a place to make you feel better about things if you choose to watch soaps or news channels. It all plays on our negative emotions and swings stressful situations into the bad stress category.

Being a modern Caveman, we still need that survival instinct. There are times when we still have to have that little 'extra' something. When we push our button, something different happens now.

We kept our ancestors' fight or flight button in the same place and wired up the same way. We have never evolved anything new or better, and we continue to use the button daily. We have the ability for the same reactions as they had when they faced their Mammoths; everything works exactly the same way, our brains have the same access to the button, and the same adrenaline and toxins are pumped into our bodies.

There are two things that have changed in today's society. One is the threat from a Woolly Mammoth. "But they are extinct!" I hear you shout. The second thing is that we have added a 'freeze' reflex. Our button now services the 'fight, flight or freeze'.

Let's talk about these Mammoths then. You may think that today there is no longer any threat from a Woolly Mammoth, but I disagree. The threat of a Mammoth is still here; they can produce the exact same fight or flight response as they did all those years ago. They can make us want to push our buttons in an instant.

There are plenty of Mammoths out there that we come in to contact with every day. We interact with them at work, at home and whilst out playing; you just do not realise what they are and where they were hiding.

The second part is that society has taught us that we are not allowed to just use the 'fight or flight' reflex. We have been taught that we also have to consider another response; the 'freeze' reaction, which is what creates our bad stress.

You are probably scratching your head thinking that I have lost the plot, but bear with me.

We have the same button that has been handed down from the Cavemen, the exact same one that I described Bert and Errol using to save their own lives in the last chapter.

How many times each day, week or month have you felt the sudden rush of adrenaline and fear run through your body? That feeling and reaction would have been something very similar to what Bert and Errol had when they came face to face with a real six-ton Woolly Mammoth. So, if there are no Mammoths, why are we still pushing our buttons?

These modern-day Mammoths trigger the same response when they make us feel that we are being threatened. So why is it not obvious that these Mammoths are out in the open?

Tip: You might want to read this next section in the style of David Attenborough; it will help.

These Mammoths are at home, at work; they are everywhere. They have developed the best use of camouflage that any animal has ever managed to master. They are champion hiders and only appear to those who they target. As soon as they have done their job, they disappear leaving the recipient human scared and irrational.

Other humans close by will not have seen this Mammoth; it was a targeted attack. They will not have even felt its presence. Other humans will be confused of the target human's reaction. They will think that the Mammoth's victim is being petty, that they are overreacting and the response is out of character. They will smile and move away, making the Mammoth's actions even more impactful as they ignore the sufferer. The other humans will then see this as a weakness and will speak about this outburst around the kitchen area or over email.

The Mammoth's pounce had its full impact, when it appeared for only a micro-second, caused its prey to hit its stress button and for the others not to have seen it. The constant talking about this secret attack by the others and making direct fun of the target human, only prolongs the effects of the Mammoth's attack, and it will plot to scare its next victim.

Looking for these Mammoths is easy when you know where to look and what you are looking for. When you are trained, you are able to see them everywhere. Then you will see that some are targeting you, while others are lining up your colleagues.

If we take a look at a normal, modern-day Caveman's daily work routine, we can pick out the potential attacks. These unsuspecting people are at work, doing their daily chores, speaking to clients, and getting on with their job. Then out of the blue, a Mammoth appears right in front of them. No one sees it coming. How did it manage to sneak up to the quarry's desk, completely undetected?

The first inkling our stooge knew about this was when they heard a normal office noise, a 'ping'. A new email has landed in our modern-day Caveman's inbox. They look at the sender and see it is from their boss.

They open the message, thinking it is another useless email, then they see it says, "Can I see you in my office ASAP?" There are no more words on the screen, the rest of it blank. They stare at the email; only those eight words appear right in front of them. Then, only for a fraction of a second, those words form the shape of a Mammoth and it scares the pants off them.

There it is, the Mammoth, showing itself and disappearing in a flash. Our victim has already started to hit their stress button. They ask the person sat next to them what they think the message means. The other person reads the same eight words, shrugs and says, "Probably nothing," not seeing any trace of the Mammoth.

Our modern-day Caveman's stress button has already been pressed. They saw the Mammoth right in front of them and they felt threatened. Their finger hit the button the moment they saw it.

Our modern-day Caveman probably thought that this is some sort of punishment coming by email. The negative world that they are used to is going to ruin their day. They expect the worst to happen and they prepare for it by pushing the button. Our Caveman is the only one that saw this threat as it was directed at them; they are the one that has to deal with it.

Hearing an instruction or reading it in an email like this, which came out of the blue, has an effect on the recipient as only they will feel the pressure from the Mammoth.

We are all hardwired the same way and most of us are used to being spoken to like this, so any other day it will not be a big surprise to our system. The Mammoth has been waiting for this one 'off day' to pounce; it saw the opportunity and took it. It jumped right in front of our poor hard-working, distracted colleague and made them push their button. Then people think this reaction is completely irrational and unwarranted but we all know it can happen to the best of us.

Our Caveman who was forced to push his button is sat at their desk, still staring at the words on the screen. There is no return from this push of the button. In a negative state, our Caveman knows where this conversation is going to head and it is all going to be bad. Their head has had a massive injection of toxins, making them think of all the awful things that could happen.

The Mammoth's next move may not have the potential to take their life, but it does intend to make it very difficult. Our Caveman is now linking work with their negative emotion. They think back and realise that no one has ever paid them a compliment, so this must be bad news.

Like most work environments (apart from the exceptional few brilliant companies), people are too busy with their own work to realise someone else is doing a good job. Praise is seldom given and any positive feedback is muted.

Our Caveman goes to work, at one of the not-so-good places, works hard, gets their job done to the best of their ability, and they believe that they do a good job.

Back to our story, our Caveman's pushing of the button has given them an instant insight into the boss's thoughts. It is going to be a one-sided conversation.

There is not going to be coffee offered, let alone the sight of a biscuit.

People can become used to these types of interactions and no longer see them as threats, but every now and again someone's guard gets dropped and the Mammoth knows it. When this happens, our natural instincts tell us that something is not right; we have no information on the matter and we are all natural worriers. We prefer to describe our negative emotions to each other rather than the good. This is why we moan about the bad situations at work, rather than the good work we all do, each and every day.

So our Caveman expects the worst. They get up and start to head towards the boss's door. They will be going through everything that they have done over the last three months, thinking "What could I have done wrong? and probably "Great, I now have to rewrite my CV."

Even before they get halfway to the office, the adrenaline designed for them to use for the fight or flight reflex is coursing through their veins. They know they are unable to lose control in the office so they just hold it in. They start to feel hot, even slightly shaky. Those toxins are making them feel sick and even ill. They have just had to use the new modern freeze reaction from the 'fight, flight or freeze'.

Those thousands of thoughts are being processed at lightning quick speeds, thanks to those toxins floating around in their head. By the time they get to the boss's door, they are a wreck; they are using all their will power to make their legs work just to keep walking. The freeze reaction is trying its hardest to get full control and make them just stand there. Our Caveman is on the verge of losing control of all emotions. What they really want to do is either run away or start fighting with the boss. They know that if they do either, it would make the boss's job so much easier and they would not get a chance to pack their desk. Instead, they force themselves to face the music.

At the boss's office threshold, they croak out, "You wanted to see me?" putting on a brave face and the best smile they can muster. Holding off the freeze response, they enter the office and close the door as a delay tactic. They are now trapped, cornered and have no idea what is going to happen next. We can all relate to having similar situations thrown at us. The main point is that the Mammoth is not actually working for our boss. It is in these situations that they make us feel that they are.

Our brave Caveman takes a chair, sits down and waits. The boss looks up from his computer screen and leans forward, giving all the signs of a pre-emptive strike. The Caveman waits for it and the boss says, "How are we getting on with that Carnaby's job? We may have some more work coming our way. How do you feel about taking more work on?"

For a second, the Caveman washes the question around in their frazzled brain. They look for the danger signs still on edge and then realised they are not going to be sacked. How are they supposed to relax and start thinking straight? They really need a lie down, but in reality all they can do is pull their thoughts back to the question and try to give a decent answer.

All those toxins and the burst of adrenaline are still surging around their body; it is waiting to be used up. They cannot unpress the button. They are sat there unable to do anything to get rid of all those nasty, last remaining toxins in their body. They no longer need these floating around in their bloodstream. They can do nothing to calm their heart rate, stop sweating and refocus their brain in order to answer the question. What they should be saying is that they are snowed under with all their own work and that the last job still needs their full attention but they want out of the office, so they just reply, "Of course." The boss smiles, pointing at the door.

Our exhausted Caveman gets up and walks out, thinking about what the hell had just happened. They have too much work on already and have just accepted another case because they were not able to think of a reason to say no. They feel cheated and all because of the Mammoth.

They were first scared by the Mammoth, leading them to believe they were about to get sacked. As they were thinking of how they could try and keep their job, the boss manages to give them extra work, without them putting up any kind of a fight.

Our Caveman sits back down at their desk and the person next to them looks over and asks if they are alright. The Caveman is so exhausted and angry but they have no idea why. They just say, "Yeah, I'm OK."

Our Caveman's work colleague accepts this as a positive response and goes back to work.

They sit there and boil for a few minutes; they get angry and emotional. Feeling stupid and hating everyone including the boss, but really it is the Mammoth's fault. It is not stupidity that they can feel, it is the Mammoth, laughing at them, and it burns.

This is where our Caveman needs a release. They are sat there in a chair, fuming, no longer needing those toxins and adrenaline, but they remain in their system. These ingredients were ready to get used. Instead their body has no choice but to try and dissolve all those harmful fluids back into the organs, tissues and biological systems. They can only get stored there as they are never going to get used again.

The control of our button is a difficult thing to master and we leave it open to get abused by our body, which it does on a regular basis.

Let's go hunt for another Mammoth. Our Caveman has just had a really bad day at work. They have just picked up more work and just want to go home. They get in the car and start the drive home. This drive should be an easy one; they have done it hundreds of times before. It is usually a time of reflection, giving them a chance to unwind before they get home to have some fun with the family.

They know there is going to be some traffic up ahead but they are used to it. As expected, on the dual carriageway, there is a line of cars in front of them. They slow and join the queue as their junction is coming up. They patiently make slow progress with the flow of traffic up to the junction.

They know that once on the junction, it is a short, easy drive home.

Bang, just at this moment when they are about to come off the dual carriageway, another Mammoth pounces. These blighters are masters of disguise and it was not seen until the last minute. It came out of nowhere and surprised our Caveman. They are exhausted, they just want to get home, but it does not stop them from pushing the button again.

This time, the Mammoth is hanging out the back window of a red BMW. It decided to push its ugly mug up against the glass of the BMW for only a moment, just as the BMW squeezes into the gap that is too small for it, right in front of our Caveman's car. This time, the Mammoth appears to be working with the BMW driver.

The BMW decided that they did not want to queue up and were going to drive down the outside lane and push in, right at the last minute, in front of our Caveman's car.

The Caveman does not have the strength to stop the button from being pressed and it is far too late as the fight or flight response has already gone into full swing.

There is little choice for our Caveman; they, along with their little car, have been threatened by an inconsiderate driver. They slam on the brakes and the BMW pulls right in front of them, not even showing a sign of thanks. The button has been pressed. The Caveman has more adrenaline and toxins pumping into their system but they cannot do anything. So they invoke the freeze response once again.

What they need to do is use up that adrenaline. Their body wants them to do something with it, get out of the car, run up to the BMW, and start fighting with the driver. There is little chance of escape as they are stuck in traffic.

All our Caveman can do is sit there, strapped in with the seatbelt. They grip the steering wheel making their knuckles go white. The only activity they are able to do is some small hand exercises but this is not enough to burn up those toxins now released into the body. These toxins again need to be reabsorbed back into the body. All those harmful substances are being stored up alongside the others, from all the previous button pressings.

Our Caveman's last stop before they get home is to pop into the shop and pick up a pint of milk for the morning. They manage to park the car close to the supermarket doors and get into the shop. They find the milk and everything is going smoothly. They are beginning to calm down a little from the BMW incident but it is still irritating them.

They walk toward the self-service till and the queue is relatively short. They pull a few coins from their pocket and expect to be back in their car very shortly.

Then another Mammoth hits them, this time coming in from the least expected place. They failed to see that the person in front of them has nothing in their hands. Instead they have been holding a place in the queue for their partner, who has just arrived with a trolley. Our Caveman catches some movement and when they look, sat under the trolley is the Mammoth. Laughing at our Caveman, it then scampers off under the till. The Mammoth moves so fast that no one sees it.

There is no choice, our poor Caveman's body is totally exhausted there is no control left. Seeing the Mammoth do this, they again hit the button. They have had their place taken in the queue by someone who cannot read the 'Express Lane' sign hanging over the till. Our Caveman cannot stop another push of the button. Bang! Their body is back in the fight or flight mode but once again they have to conform and force themselves not to react.

The heart rate shoots up and again they start to feel hot and angry. They want to grab that trolley and shove it out of the way, which will probably start a fight. Their body welcomes this as it's ready for it. They might feel the need to run forward and jump in front of these impolite shoppers, but this would be another fight waiting to happen. Their button is telling them to do all these things, their mind going through a thousand smart sayings to justify these actions. However, being brought up knowing that society will not tolerate these shopping indiscretions, they again resort to the freeze response.

Nurture has taught our Caveman that it is not polite to start a fight over milk. They want to be allowed back into this shop again. They swallow hard and have to calm themselves, reabsorbing those last toxins back into the body as they watch the trolley be unloaded in front of them. Biting their tongue, they force themselves to pay and then walk out to their car before doing anything.

Again, the sting left by that last Mammoth hurts; it has built up throughout the day, and now it is personal. Our Caveman gets in the car and screams, "Why me?" There is no physical exertion to burn off those toxins; they just get reabsorbed.

These examples show where these blasted critters hide. These are just a few of the places where we can find our modern-day Mammoths lurking. They are everywhere; they hide in letters from people like the tax man, personal emails from the credit card companies, and my personal favourite, the "sorry we missed you" cards left in the letterbox by the postie.

All of these hiding places have been designed and tested by the Mammoth. They are able to hide and wait for their prey. They can wait days, weeks, even months, before they pounce. They disappear as quickly as they arrive, and long before anyone else can see them.

These sneaky Mammoths have had years of practice. They know when to hit us, when our guard is down. They force us to push the button, then to rub salt in the wound, they stay close by so we can sense them watching and laughing at us, before we lose our control.

4. DON'T PUSH THE BUTTON

How can you and others help?

I love a great story, so to highlight the issue of some people making us want to push our buttons, let's talk about an ex-soldier. There was once an ex-soldier who lived in a modest home on a beautiful beach. He had a loving family and a small fishing boat. He lived to fish, and every day he woke up happy. Each day, he would get into his boat and go out to sea, fishing for tuna. He became so good, that on every trip he was able to bring back enough tuna to feed his entire family and still have plenty to sell at the local market. He would trade and sell his catch, and make more than enough money to buy the things he needed for his lifestyle.

One day, an American walked past the market stall and saw the man's catch of tuna. The American started to talk to the man and he discovered the man's story of what he did, where he lived and of his knowledge about being able to catch tuna. The American knew that with this man's fishing ability, he could make both him and the fisherman some serious money.

He spoke to the man, offering a chance for him to work with the American. The American stated that he was an expert in business, that he had an education second to none. He stated that his business sense would allow the man to grow a business quickly, and with the American's investment, he could be running an entire fleet of fishing boats catching tuna every day. The ex-soldier could be hauling in huge amounts of fish and earning large sums of money, which they would share.

If the man was prepared to work the long hours with the American advising him, he could one day earn enough money to retire, and he would be able to buy a house on the beach and carry out his favourite pastime every day. The ex-soldier could have enough money to feed his family and be able to relax whenever he wanted to.

The ex-solider smiled and asked if the American's education was expensive. The American grew by a few inches stating that it cost his father a lot of money. Slightly intrigued, the American asked, "Why do you ask about my schooling?"

The man replied, "No reason but is it too late to ask for a refund?"

This story tells how some people are willing to exploit others, offering them exactly what they had in the first place. Not every offer or opportunity will have a good ending. It may be hard to spot but there are quite a few potential Mammoths lurking within this story.

These Mammoths would probably appear as soon as the ex-soldier started to consider the American's offer. The American genuinely believed he could help the ex-soldier and he would not have intended for a Mammoth to spring out.

The ex-soldier, however, knew that his life was fulfilled. He did not take the bait to 'improve' his life and did not see the need to do anything that would set off his button. He did not jump on the offer to become wealthy. He was comfortable with his life and was able to control the urge to make an irrational decision, thereby bypassing those Mammoths.

The American was obviously not thinking that he was going to drop a herd of Mammoths on the ex-soldier as he only thought he would be helping this poor man. The American was asking his only question; who wants to fish every day in a tiny boat? Instead of seeing how the ex-soldier saw his life, the American was thinking of himself, justifying this by believing he was doing it for the ex-soldier.

He thought that if he put the effort in to helping this fisherman, then he should get something back as well. A point to note: not everyone sees wealth as having lots of money. Some people put money before happiness, just like this American did in this story.

When individuals do not consider other people's thoughts or beliefs, rushing into doing something that they consider to be worthy, they are in actual fact making hiding places for the Mammoth. We can all relate to someone thinking that they are helping and all they caused was stress and confusion. The best way to deal with a (un)helpful person is not to accept the offer; graciously decline just like our ex-soldier.

Being comfortable with what we do, only pushing ourselves when we want to, will create more happiness and less opportunity for a Mammoth attack.

Watching out for modern-day Mammoths is not an easy thing. Every person will probably deal with a small amount of stress in their life, but it has to be under their control. When people hand over control to someone else, like a boss or a needy friend (or a greedy American), this is when the button can be abused.

A lurking Mammoth can hide in someone's best intentions. Remember, they will only show themselves to their prey for a fraction of a second. The most sincere, kindest person in the world can offer help in something that they believe will assist. That Mammoth pouncing will trigger an unwanted response by the recipient towards them and their kind actions. During these times, the Mammoth will prolong the pain, as now when things have calmed a little, an apology will be needed. The Mammoth's sneakiness is not to be underestimated.

People never think about the impact of their actions on others; that quick one-liner email, poorly typed and sent without a second thought, can have people pushing their buttons within seconds. That simple sentence can easily hide a Mammoth and it can launch a full-scale attack on the recipient when they read it. The writer of the email, who is completely unaware that they have included the Mammoth, will blame the reader for 'reading it wrong'. The reader being the only person to have seen the Mammoth finds it hard to justify their response and they end up taking the blame by apologising. The Mammoth watches from a distance laughing to itself, then hides once again.

Every press of our button causes upset, taking valuable minutes from our day. It makes us have negative thoughts and requires us to gain control, and only then can we calm ourselves. In modern society, we choose the freeze approach over the fight or flight response. Each unwanted button press is a stealer of our time, our sanity and our strength.

The effort we put into calming ourselves after each press is immense. There is no wonder we arrive home completely exhausted. It's not the 10 hours that we have just spent at work that is making us want to crash on the sofa. It is the constant pressing of our buttons that causes us the fatigue. We all know that at the end of a stressful day, we do not want to do anything other than sit in front of the TV or go to bed.

If our modern-day Cavemen from the previous chapter were to count the number of times they pushed their button every day, it would probably be in the double figures. In comparison, our ancestors probably only pushed their buttons once or twice a day and, more importantly, when they pushed the button, they ran around burning off those toxins and then rested afterwards.

Each push of the button takes away some control over the future use of it. The strength needed to resist another push fades throughout the day as we tire from the constant Mammoth attacks. By the end of a busy day, we can no longer prevent another push. Each push causes our stress levels to rise and each trivial situation becomes more stressful than the last. All the Mammoths will find their job getting easier and easier throughout the day.

Every press of the button is a stress 'event' recorded in our modern-day Caveman's daily diary. These daily Mammoth sightings and attacks make the pushing of the button harder to control. The same type of stress event should be easier to control. However, as we are so busy, we are unable to learn from the button press and it just gets compounded; like a well-used light switch, less pressure is needed each time you use it.

All of these presses release the adrenaline and those toxins, pumping them into the body, which should be used for the immediate physical exertion, and not being stored in delicate tissues as it is not healthy.

Our bodies are designed to use the button when it is required. It is all part of modern-day living. What has not been factored in is the rest period required after each press and the opportunity to allow the body to remove these dangerous chemicals. The body is an amazing contraption. If it is given time, it will repair and expel nasty, unwanted substances.

If you are nodding your head and relate to these presses, then we need to talk about a medical condition called 'Chronic Stress'.

This illness comes from people who push their buttons far too many times, living with the bad stuff in their systems for too long and without any periods of rest. The fact that you are reading this book means there is a high chance that you live with stress. You should now understand where stress comes from and know a reason why you have to control and reduce it.

These toxins, which were designed to save our lives, are now slowly killing us. Our muscles and organs have been absorbing high doses of these harmful fluids. They are stored like nuclear waste, which needs long periods of time to become safe. If we manage these levels of toxins properly, then they are expelled before they do any damage. But if we keep adding to these levels, most of our organs and body tissue will keep hold of it and it will slowly destroy the good tissue.

The body was designed to absorb one or two button hits a day. Our busy, hectic lifestyle overloads our system and cause a mass build-up of these toxins in our organs.

Our Caveman ancestors, who designed this button, never had to contend with rush hour traffic or losing reception on their mobile phones, so did not think about putting in any safety switches.

Stress is one of the main causes of many modern-day health problems and if it was not the cause of it, then it will certainly become a complication which prolongs or worsens any illness. Stress has already been linked to overeating, overdrinking (alcoholism), depression, anxiety and sleep disorders.

There is a growing number of studies that suggest stress can cause early heart disease. It can start, aid or excel the growth of cancerous cells, and it can create blood pressure problems, which is a concern on its own. If you do not believe me, look up the research carried out by the CIPD (Chartered Institute of Personnel and Development) or the APA (American Psychological Association). There are hundreds of studies on the internet each blaming stress for countless illnesses.

So what if none of these conditions concern you? Then the next ones might. It can affect your appearance, it can produce greasy skin, and it can be the cause of acne, even causing early hair loss.

The best of these conditions, which I have saved until last, is that it can reduce and even kill our sex drive. Yep, you heard that right, no more coitus.

This last buzzkill can be the downfall in our lives. Relationships can end because of this one factor. Partners can be forced into the arms of others as they feel unloved and ignored. No one (which includes the sufferer) will see that this is all because of the lack of control and the constant use of their stress button.

We can all see a rash, a bruise or an arm in plaster, and can sympathise with the sufferer. We can sometimes see that we are overweight and struggling with our appearance. But no one can see stress. It is invisible; people do see the sufferer as an irate, angry, mean individual, who does not deserve their attention.

We do not recognise this truly life-sucking parasite is attached to us. We wave it off as a normal everyday occurrence. It takes up too much of our time and effort to try and control it, and we turn into stress monsters which get ignored.

We try to avoid stress, but we end up dealing with it. If we are not dealing with it, then we are thinking about it. Stress is now a troublesome daily life occurrence for everyone. It needs to be dealt with before we are all in serious trouble and we make the health service buckle under the pressure of our ignorance of what our stressful lives are doing to us. We can all feel stressed at times, and because it has become such a 'norm', we have no reason to tackle this unseen potential downfall that comes of the modern-day Caveman. We need to wake up, see the damage stress is causing to us, and recalibrate our thinking of it.

Let's do a simple test. There are no trick questions, you just need to answer them honestly. Do not think too much about them. If you do not want to write in the book, then you can download these tests from my website:

www.carlrosierjones.com

Question	Demands	Yes	No
1	Do you worry about performance targets and deadlines more often than not?		
2	Do you have too many people relying on you?		
3	Are there conflicts between work and home?		
4	Have you got too much work to do?		
5	Do you find you work longer hours just to catch up?		
	Total		

Now if you have three or more "Yes's" then I am sorry to say but there will be signs of stress in your life. Let's dig a little deeper with another little test.

Question	Control	Yes	No
1	Do you take time for regular breaks?		
2	Can you ignore things that are not in your control?		
3	Do you have the ability to say 'No'?		
4	Has your day been Mammoth Free?		
5	Have you pressed your button less than three times today?		
	Total		

How many "No's" have you scored? Do I have to point out the obvious? I can hear people say, "Yes, but..." and it is easy for me to type, "It's all in your control." However, I won't.

Being a Police Officer, I know there are demands that cannot be ignored. However, it is easier to work smarter than to work harder. Let's try one more. I promise this will be the last one... for this chapter, anyway.

Question	Lifestyle	Yes	No
1	Do you drink alcohol every night?		
2	Do you chill on the sofa every night?		
3	Do you rant rather than have a calm conversation?		
4	Do you think you are overweight?		
5	Do you eat junk food instead of proper meals, rather than just as a treat?		
	Total		

Add up your "Yes's". If you have over three, then stress is a big part of your lifestyle.

From the three simple checklists above, I would guess that you have put four to five yes's or no's in each set of boxes. Put all the three questionnaires together, and the impact of having a stressful life is easy to see.

I could have put 20 questions in each box but the results would have all been the same, except that you would have been bored completing all the questions for the same result. The results are only to show whether you are stressed or not, and if you are, whether you want to take action.

You may want to start with a few handy sayings or mantras to use every day. If you want to start thinking more positively about life, consider using these;

- Life will always be too short; you will always want just one more day.
- Just because you are busy, you are not necessarily being productive.
- Thinking and doing are two very different things.
- We all get the opportunity to live the lives we can create.
- It all happens for a reason.
- Some people we are never going to get on with; accept it and work around them.
- An apology is not necessary before you can forgive.
- There are two days this week that we will never be able to make a difference – yesterday and tomorrow.

OK, so we know we are stressed! We have come to terms with the fact that we are not in control of our buttons. After the acceptance stage, next comes the denial stage or the blame stage. There are bound to be some questions people will start asking;

- If all this button ever does is cause stress, why do we still need it?
- If we now only invoke the freeze response and cannot use the fight or flight actions, surely the button is redundant?
- With the potential harm it can cause, why shouldn't we just get it taken out? Then the Mammoth can jump out whenever it likes and we won't have to worry about any reaction.

This stage is relatively short-lived once people come to terms that this is our body. This is millions of years of evolution, but it has only been since the 1980s (ish) that stress is such a major player in our busy lives. We need to remind ourselves that the button has proven to be a wonderful and a very powerful tool in many positive situations, and only then can we can move on to the next stage.

This is where all the work needs to be done, including understanding the problem stage, which is not blaming the button itself. The acceptance of a lack of control we have over our buttons is the issue.

We have handed over one of our body's most natural responses to other people. They are free to use and abuse our button whenever they want.

We have relinquished control, probably because we have been taught that we have to concentrate on other less important things, or we have followed others when they have handed power to other people, learning to do the same.

Another concern is that people do not acknowledge that we live in a materialistic world, mixed with our negative society. If you consider that most people are probably happy doing a responsible job and are happy being paid a reasonable wage for it, why do they worry about money? I would guess that it is because they want something more.

I know I said there would be no personal stories at the beginning of this book, but many years ago I wanted promotion. I became fully qualified and worked towards building a portfolio of evidence to prove that I could move into the next rank. I became blinded, as I was so focused on promotion I had forgotten to enjoy myself. My drive to make it to the next rank alienated me from my friends and family. I became a cold, unapproachable individual who did a fantastic job and held a lot of support from the people who I thought mattered: my bosses. I handed my button over to them. They made me dance to their tune and hit my button as many times as they liked.

After a few years of chasing promotion, I had to stop and reassess what I was actually trying to achieve. I was exhausted and could not understand why I had not been promoted. I had done everything that was asked of me but I kept failing my final interview. The reason was simple; my bosses loved me for the results I brought in. My interview board had a good write-up from my immediate boss, but I did not come across as a good manager during my hour-long dialogue.

After questioning myself, I found the question that answered why I kept failing my board. I asked myself, "Why do I want it?" This was the question I should have asked a few years back to save myself a lot of upset and all those button presses.

My answer to the question was simple; more money and more respect. I contemplated this answer for a while, trying to work out why it was wrong. Why was this answer not enough to get me promoted? Then one day, I stumbled over the correct answer. The reason someone who wants to get promoted should never be for the money, and it should never be for the status.

Promotion is for people who want to take on extra responsibility and make other people's lives better.

Once this has been achieved, only then will they earn the extra money and gain the kudos that I desired. The whole drive for me, and probably many others, was the money. I wanted more money so I could buy a motorbike or to go on better holidays; it was not to make other people's lives better. I had endured years of someone else pushing my button, me giving control to them and causing a whole lot of misery during that time.

The materialist urge had taken a hold of me and I needed to shake it off. I stepped away from promotion and reassessed what I wanted in my life. If I wanted the extra money and the extra status, then I had to do something that I felt was worthwhile, something worthy of my effort and where I could control my own button.

A study by a bunch of psychologists at the University of Warwick looked at 1,000 people who had been promoted, and were able to show that the higher up in an organisation someone has been able to climb, the worse their mental health became.

They stated that each time someone got promoted, they gained about 10% extra stress and because of their status and not wanting to be seen as weak, they reduced their visits to a doctor by 20%. They believed this extra pressure came from the increased workload, the extra responsibility and reduced leisure time.

Professor Oswald (no, not the one from *Spiderman*) stated that his team believed that there was no physical benefits at all in gaining a promotion; however, they believed it can have an impact on mental health.

My observations have been that the more control someone has in their daily work, being able to make decisions or pass them to someone who can, the less stress they have. When someone takes responsibility for others in a managerial role, they then lose that control, and when it goes wrong, it is them who have every decision scrutinised and checked, increasing the stress.

This want for promotion comes with it the extra pay. However, the extra stress and potential for stress-related illness needs to be balanced. People who choose to be promoted are electing to walk a more dangerous path, putting more potential Mammoths in their way.

I have always wanted to help others, hence why I have worn so many hats, but I decided promotion was not right for me. This decision led me to start exploring and creating the Caveman Principles.

Our world has a massive impact on modern-day Cavemen. With unforgiving bosses and unreasonable clients, it has turned the original Cave dweller into a stressed individual who now lives their life on a knife's edge.

A new belief has also crept into the Caveman's head, and this is that everyone is incompetent. We no longer work in selected teams; many of us are multi-tasking and not working with the same people regularly. We all want to get the job done and we all know how best to complete any task. Stress creeps in when we are part of an unknown team, and we argue over how it should be done.

I know how I operate at work. I am a 'get in there and see what we have got' sort of operator. Others prefer to gather all the information and delay doing anything positive until they have a plan. When I have to work with these sort of people, I not only press my button, I hold it down. Sometime you may see me physically shake with the amount of stuff that is being pumped into my system. These interactions have such massive stress implications that I have written the next few chapters just to help and explain these interactions. Keeping a rigid work practice will mean that others who do not follow these rules, will be seen as stupid, that they are attacking others with their stupidity and this will set off the button. Their stupidity cannot be corrected as they will be thinking the exact same thing of the other person. Neither will relent and both will attack and defend their position.

I can go on giving example after example of how the button is pressed. I have given enough of them for you to recognise the ignition of a stressful event. So moving on, how can a modern-day Caveman combat this stress thing?

One way to fight against the abuse of our button is to stop the freeze response and take back more control of it. Remember, the Mammoth is sneaky, it is a creature of habit, but it is not very bright. Once it has found a good hiding place, it will use it again and again. If you have ever grabbed hold of an electric fence, I bet you will do everything to avoid doing it again, (unless you want to be on YouTube), so why do we keep going back to the Mammoth's same hiding place?

We need to identify their hideouts and start to avoid them, finding a new route through the Mammoth minefield. It will take dedication and some effort. Using a diary, write out the stressful times you find yourself in each and every day. If you boil down the problem, the triggering of your button will probably be the same thing time and again. Whether at work it is the same person, the same client, the same contractor or the same unreasonable demand, there will be a common element here.

At home, do the same. Is it the same neighbour, the same argument or the demands on your time?

Learn them, recognise them, approach them from a different direction. Try new ways of communicating or just accepting it for what it is. Do everything to prepare yourself, but if nothing else, just try to avoid them.

If we are prepared to look for the common hiding spots of the Mammoths, we can start to do something positive, preparing a response and stopping the freezing reaction from happening. The more Mammoths we can avoid, the more control we will gain over our response and our button. Once this step has been accomplished, we will know that not all Mammoths can be avoided, but we have dramatically reduced our exposure to them. The more advanced Caveman can start to recognise the initial feelings of when the fight or flight button wants to be pressed.

Once we reduce the exposure to Mammoths, we will have more strength and we can use this to reduce the other pushes. This is a skill, and with all skills, the more practice we have, the better we will become.

With this extra strength and recognition of this condition, we might not be able to stop the button from being hit, but we use the energy to make the length of time it is depressed shorter, and therefore reducing the amount of toxins getting into our system.

Cavemen are all different; what works for one may not work for another. Some Cavemen develop a sense of humour being able to laugh at their Mammoths. This can be dangerous as it can be seen as being unprofessional but doing this takes an amazing amount of power back. Other Cavemen can prepare for the attack. They can guess where the Mammoth might be hiding and appear to toughen up. Then when the Mammoth pounces, they do not freeze, they are able to stare it down. Some have been able to completely ignore them. Other Cavemen have even made peace with their Mammoths and have started to say that all Mammoths are not bad. These are also known as the 'Zen' Mammoth masters.

People can make honest mistakes and we can all think the worst of people, but when they are busy, they can be focused on the wrong thing, especially when they are in a hurry. Modern-day Cavemen cannot control everything, and sometimes these things just need to be acknowledged and ignored.

When others send a poorly-worded email, miss a junction whilst they are driving, or get into the wrong queue, do not look at it as a Mammoth attack.

There will always be rude and impatient bullies out there, but think about it; they are in the minority. They spoil our outlook on life through their own selfishness. Modern-day Cavemen need to start to relax more, not to expect the worst from everyone.

Cavemen need to start thinking more positively, and one way is to communicate in a more positive way. Try to stop using negative words and see what happens. Instead of saying 'but,' use the word 'and';

So you want to use the blue one, but I was going to use that colour.

So you want to use the blue one, and I was going to use that colour.

Both phrases give the same sentiment and deliver the same message, however there is no sting in the second sentence. Try not to use the word 'don't' as the human brain does not hear this word.

Adults have had to try and recognise this word as it does not form a natural instruction. When a child hears, "Don't drop that," or, "Don't put that doughnut in the CD player," they actually hear an instruction, forgetting the negative at the start of it. They hear "drop that" and "put the doughnut in the CD player."

It is the same for adults when we have been expressly forbidden to do something by using the word 'don't' at the beginning of a sentence. When a long instruction has finished, we have forgotten the first word and how it started. When giving an instruction, make it a positive statement instead. Ask what you want someone to do, rather than what you 'don't' want them to do.

We are all in this thing called life, and there is only one way out of it. Make it a worthwhile and happy experience. Like attracts like, so if a Cavemen creates small pockets of trust and forgiving, others will join the group. A Caveman's life will become easier and we can turn a negative, nasty environment into a happy, relaxed and more productive one. More importantly, we can choose who wants to be in our tribe.

Stress is all about being in control. When we have no control of the number of Mammoths we meet every day, we do not have control on how we deal with them.

We all have the ability to recognise a Mammoth. They want to work against us and rub us up the wrong way. They can ruin our lives if we let them. We have the ability to communicate and we have compassion, so use them both in a positive way.

We must stop thinking the worst of people. We have to be more positive and more accepting of mistakes and change the ways we interact with 'stupid' people. We have choices, but it is up to you to want to make a difference.

The next section of this book, Part 2, will help you manage stress better by understanding the people in your tribe. To control your stress even more, you can learn how to understand and handle change, which follows in Part 3.

If you want less stress and are prepared to make the journey to change your life, only the first few steps are the scary ones.

PART TWO

PEOPLE WHO THINK THEY KNOW
EVERYTHING ARE A GREAT ANNOYANCE
TO THOSE OF US WHO DO.

ISAAC ASIMOV

5. PEOPLE PROFILING

We all want to fit into a box.

People profiling is not just how someone looks when they stand sideways on. Profiling is when an individual can identify a personal trait in another. Identifying and using these traits can reduce conflict and can win arguments. The key to successful profiling is to listen to all words in a conversation, watch body movements and go with your instincts.

This part of the book is where we can start to have some proper fun. There is no right or wrong way to profile anyone. You do not need to be frightened, just give it a go; it is a lot of fun, and when we get it right, it can make a real difference. Understanding this dark art can start to unravel the mystery of why some people can be of real help and good company, whilst with others we are thinking that a hit man may want to pay them a visit.

Profiling people is a skill and again with any skill, practicing it will make you a better judge of character. I have used personality profiling many times in my job. The ability to work out how a person thinks, operates and responds can be a huge advantage in my line of work.

Profiling is an important tool that is no longer given any credit in today's world. Most of us take people at 'face' value. We are just too busy to dig a little deeper and cannot see the point of working someone out for the sake of being nice. When we ignore this skill, we allow true opportunities and potential lifelong friends to pass straight through our busy lives.

We have all done it when we meet someone new and instantly hit it off with them. We exchange details, swap phone numbers and invite them round to our house for a drink and a social. There is 'something' there that makes us want to spend time getting to know them better, but we do not question what that 'something' is.

On the other occasions, there are the 'others'. The ones we want to punch within two seconds of meeting them, and then we cannot wait to get away. Again, we do not overanalyse these things, and move on to our next appointment.

Some chance encounters can be easy to dismiss, especially those in our personal lives. However, in work or in the course of our business, we can be missing important information on how to deal with these exchanges.

We are never going to get on with everyone, as some of these people can push our buttons within seconds. Some of them we can ignore, others we have to work with.

If you could learn how to read someone, to place a label on them, naming their personality; would that help? Then learning how to interact with those labels, understanding how they think, communicate and interact; would that make life easier? How about once you have labelled and understood how you can manage them better; would all of this help reduce your own stress?

It is time to dust off your old Dymo machine as it's time to start labelling. Have you noticed that your likeable people all seem to have the same personality traits? Whether they are outward, quiet or plain crazy? Have you thought about the ones who we despise? They all seem to have the same traits.

Does your stress Mammoth only appear when you deal with those certain types of people, mainly the ones you do not get on with?

Profiling people has gone on for hundreds and thousands of years. It is normally carried out by psychoanalysts and doctors; most of their theories are fascinating with very useful and insightful conclusions. The reason no one outside of their profession reads their theories are because you need a truck to get the manuscript home and then another to carry the dictionary to interpret them with. They fall into the heavy reading documents and use far too many big words to make it a pleasant read.

For the 'Gatherers' reading this, and those with an interest in personality profiling, the next few pages are going to be of great interest to you.

For the 'Hunters' (who have probably already left this chapter), you may want to jump ahead a few pages. This level of detail will send you round the twist.

It is always good to start at the beginning with some history. About 2,000 years ago, there lived a man. Back then, they could pronounce his name. Hippocrates was a very famous Greek physician. He liked to put people into boxes. He described people having one of his four humours and he then linked them to one of the four elements.

- Sanguine traits were linked to Air. He stated these people are lively, social, carefree, talkative and pleasure seekers.
- Choleric traits have been linked to Fire. These are excitable, impulsive and restless people with an aggressive side.
- Melancholic traits are more Earthy. These people are serious, cautious and of the suspicious type.
- Phlegmatic traits are linked to Water. These individuals are more thoughtful, private, calm and reasonable people.

Since Hippocrates published his thoughts on labelling people, there have been very few new developments in the field. Most new theories have come from the early 1900s and more recently the beginning of the second millennium.

There are a few very noteworthy people I feel should be mentioned here. A well-known Swiss psychiatrist and psychotherapist in the 1920s, whose name gets uttered in every psychology lesson around the world, started his own shoehorning theories, Carl Gustav Jung. He published his book on psychological types, describing his own four noted functions. He described that people experienced the world through sensation, intuition, feeling and thinking.

Then he divided people into more boxes, whether they were introverted or extroverted, rational (judgemental) or irrational (perceiving).

In 1928, William Moulton Marston created another, what is now known as the DISC assessment and still used in some companies for recruiting the right candidate. Never let it be said that he was a boring brain boffin, as from his own mind, he created the super-heroine, Wonder Woman. For a white-coated geek, he created and dressed a female superhero in one of the most iconic uniforms that has stood the test of time. Back to his geekiness, he also designed and built the first Polygraph machine (the lie detector), but that's more for a pub quiz book than one on stress.

His DISC idea gave people a view of themselves and how they face daily situations. His labels sometimes make me think he came up with the idea of Wonder Woman first.

- Dominance – More powerful with an unfavourable environment outlook.
- Inducement – More powerful with a favourable environment outlook.
- Submission – Less powerful with a favourable environment outlook.
- Compliance – Less powerful with an unfavourable environment outlook.

One of the best known theories for defining people, putting individuals into their own box, was created by a mother and daughter team, the Myers-Briggs Type Indicator. They created the MBTI in 1962, using Carl Jung's original theories and combining them with their own take on things, creating 16 personality types. For the psychology student reading this, let us take a stroll down memory lane. People were squashed into smaller boxes, and they were;

- ESTJ – Extraversion (E), Sensing (S), Thinking (T), Judgment (J).
- INFP – Intorversion (I), iNtuition (N), Feeling (F), Perception (P).

Then these were combined to make the Myers-Briggs codes.

- Introverted Thinking: INTPs and ISTPs
- Introverted Intuition: INFJs and INTJs
- Introverted Feeling: INFPs and ISFPs
- Introverted Sensing: ISTJs and ISFJs
- Extraverted Feeling: ENFJs and ESFJs
- Extraverted Thinking: ENTJs and ESTJs
- Extraverted iNtuition: ENFPs and ENTPs
- Extraverted Sensing: ESFPs and ESTPs

One other person, who is worth mentioning here, is David Keirsey. His work on the subject is one my favourites. In his 1978 book, he showed how to work people out using his Keirsey Temperament Sorter. He pushed people into some great names, those being;

- Artisans
- Guardians
- Idealists
- Rationals

Finally, the last person who is getting a mention is the one who gave colours to these peoples' personality traits. He was Don Lowry, who did this back in 1979. He used Gold, Orange, Green and Blue.

For at least 2,000 years, different people have shoved people into the same four boxes, describing similar personality traits in each box. All these theories have been incredibly helpful, giving me an understanding of people that I have used in my everyday job to get some quite spectacular results. All these theories have helped to form the basis of my own shoe boxing method, the Caveman Principles.

6. USING THE CTS FOR THE PEOPLE IN OUR TRIBE

We all have a role to play in our tribe.

Hunters can rejoin us here. Now that we are all back together again, it is time for a bit more fun. This is where you turn into crowd watching, psychoanalysis experts.

The CTS (Caveman Tribe Sorter) is a very simple process. Anyone who uses it will identify other people's personality traits. From these traits, we put a label on someone and treat them according to that label. Labels can be changed, amended and even removed. The important thing is to give it a go.

Labels are given to people through the CTS, for the roles that they perform in our tribes. The labels will read Hunter, Protector, Gatherer or Healer. Once someone has a label with a role on it, you will be able to communicate with them better, improve relationships and, more importantly, reduce stress.

But what if you get it wrong? Two things to be said: do not use the word 'but' and secondly, there is no room for 'what if's'. Never be afraid of putting a label on someone.

Put them into a role and see what happens. If you think you got it wrong, labels and roles can be changed; there will be no harm done. The more we practice, the better we will get at doing it right the first time.

The best person to profile someone is the one who will be asking the questions. Self-perception can often get distorted and should not be relied on. If you ask someone what they think of themselves, their reply will not be the same as what society thinks of them.

A perfect example of a distorted self-perception is to ask if someone is a good driver and then listen to their response. Everyone believes they are the best driver in the world and if someone challenges their driving or tells them that they have picked up a bad practice, it will instantly irritate them. The reason for this is that our self-perception tells us that we are great drivers and no one is allowed to criticise us. I have had to deal with many motoring offences in my work and have seen this exact thing many times. It became obvious that it was not the ticket that the offending motorist disliked, it was what the ticket represented, which was the criticism of their driving.

When asked about any character trait, people will give a response that they feel would put them into a more favourable light. It's that self-perception thing again. People are not honest with themselves and this is why it is always good to get a second opinion from someone who is a better judge of our character.

We also have to bear in mind, the age-old argument of Nature verses Nurture. This is where a person's true personality can become covered up by an expectation placed on them by their family, their job or their education. An example of Nature vs Nature is when we try to label someone with a military background into a CTS role. They might present themselves as one type but are actually someone completely different, all because of their training. They might even shoehorn themselves into one of the roles that they think they should be in. When the years of drill and discipline are finally wiped away, their true personality traits can be identified and then they are given their proper role in the tribe.

The most important thing to do is to have a go and make it a fun thing to do. Share the CTS with others and get them involved; it makes profiling people easier when others do it with you.

The first question that needs to be asked about any person that you want to categorise is; Are they an 'Open' or 'Closed' individual?

Question	CTS Part 1 – Open or Closed?	Yes	No
1	Do they talk about themselves a lot?		
2	Do they have opinions that they want to share?		
3	Are they approachable?		
4	Can you tell what they are thinking?		
5	Can you read their reactions?		
6	Are they likely to respond to a personal question?		
7	Do you think you can trust your judgement of them on face value alone?		
	Total		

Part one of the test is simple; no tricky questions and it is a simple yes or no response. Adding up the totals will show who is open and who is closed. If the number of "Yes's" outnumber the number of "No's" then that person is considered to be open. If not, then they are of closed character.

Open people are normally quite approachable; they have an easy personality and people know a lot about them. Being closed is the exact opposite. Closed individuals are the ones who people are normally wary around. They are the ones that are given a wide berth.

The second CTS question to ask is; Are they Direct or Indirect with people?

Question	CTS Part 2 – Direct or Indirect?	Yes	No
1	Do they say what they mean?		
2	Do they get straight to the point of a conversation?		
3	When they ask a question, is it normally a yes or no reply that they want?		
4	Do they tell people what they need?		
5	Can they give a straight no without giving an explanation?		
6	Do they normally go for the truth rather than spare someone's feelings?		
7	Do they take conversations literally without looking for hidden meanings?		
	Total		

Part two of the CTS is a little more difficult. The trick to answering these questions is not to dissect the question in certain situations. Keep it simple and straightforward; it is either a yes or a no.

If there are more "Yes's" than "No's" then the person is a direct communicator, and if there are more "No's" then they are indirect communicators.

If someone is a direct communicator, they will not mince their words; they appear not to care what people think when they speak their mind. If they have something to say, they will say it. If they have to give an instruction, they would get to the point and tell it 'how it is'.

Indirect people are less forceful and more tactful people. They will be concerned about other people's perceptions and emotions. They do not like to say things that would upset others. They would rather take a side than give an opinion. If they have to give an instruction, they ask it nicely and it is inserted into part of a conversation.

Now that we know how to tell if a person is Open or Closed, Direct or Indirect, we have to put them into CTS. We will then be able to give them their very own label, with a role in the tribe.

Open & Direct People
are Hunters.

Closed & Direct People
are Protectors

Closed and Indirect People
are Gatherers.

Open and Indirect People
are Healers.

7. HUNTERS

It will all work out in the end.

Hunters are Open and Direct, and of the four basic elements, they are the closest to the Air element. Looking back at our ancestral Caveman, we would have seen the Hunter telling everyone how important they were, that they were the gel that held the tribe together. These Cavemen were the main Hunters, hence the name. They would have been the fearless ones, going out of the cave to hunt for dangerous animals, so that the tribe could survive. They were willing to put their lives on the line and wanted the respect that went with that commitment. They would have been the wannabe celebrities of their time. They would have needed a big farewell as they left for a hunt and wanting a bigger hero's welcome when they returned.

There is no doubt that our Caveman Hunters, living so dangerously all the time, would have been the jokers of the tribe. When they were not out hunting, they would have needed to entertain themselves. For fun, they would have thought it was funny to have pushed a young sabre-toothed tiger into a cave where their mother-in-law was sitting, just to laugh at the response.

They would have seen this as having a little bit of harmless fun and would find it hilarious listening to her screaming and banging around as she chased it out of the cave. When the Hunters were being chastised for doing this, they would have defended their actions by saying it was just a bit of fun and not understanding the other person's upset.

Hunters were the lively ones of the group, but when they had a task, such as hunting, they would have been totally focused on the hunt. They lived their lives on results and they would have become really upset if someone was not up to their standards meaning they missed their prey. They were quick thinkers, being able to think on their feet, ready to react, constantly monitoring and reassessing their situation. The more dangerous the situation became, the better they were at finding new ways of doing things. They did not hunt by a set of rules. Things could change in a moment's notice and they needed their decisions to be more fluid, like the air. Whilst they hunted Mammoths, they knew there were too many variables that a set of

rules would never be flexible enough, so they preferred to work things out as they went along.

Back to the present day, apart from a few extra feet in height and maybe less body hair (although sometimes I am not so sure this is the case after getting into showers at the gym, but never mind), not much has changed for the modern-day Caveman. Today's Hunter is still a massive part of our tribe. Although they may not be out hunting for Mammoths, they will have found an important job that they want the same recognition for.

Hunters are inventive and enthusiastic about anything new and exciting. They are the carefree, open individuals who can talk to anyone about anything.

They seem to have no fear and appear to throw caution to the wind, which is not actually true as they are incredibly rational about their own fear and the presence of danger. Hunters just perceive danger in a very different and unique way to everyone else; they are more accustomed to Mammoth attacks and have a higher threshold of what they think is dangerous. Most daredevils will be Hunters, as will most of the extreme sports enthusiasts. They can rationalise and assess situations astonishingly quickly.

This is why they are the first to accept any challenge as their confidence in their assessment of their abilities is incredibly high.

Hunters need to have fun and are always looking for new opportunities. Whether it is a new hobby or pastime, they will throw themselves into this new obsession, until they get bored and want to find a new one. A Hunter needs to have a hobby that delivers quick wins. Everything that they start will be with enthusiasm. If, however, the hobby requires years of training, it will find its way into the garage, along with the rest of the old hobbies, sporting equipment and incomplete projects.

A Hunter needs to be stimulated daily and would even be tempted to poke a hornet's nest (physically and metaphorically) if they thought it would entertain them. Hunters appear to have no boundaries; they have no problem playing practical jokes on people they know and complete strangers. They want people to laugh at their pranks as they see it as a service, expecting lots of praise for raising morale.

Hunters can be seen as 'loose cannons' rolling around a ship's deck, wreaking havoc and destruction on anything getting in their way. They live for the 'moment' and always in the 'here and now'. They can be seen as not being serious, as they appear not to be planning for anything.

They look forward to the future and are not interested in the past. This can infuriate others as Hunters want to keep moving forward. Hunters hate debriefing for any learning opportunities made from their mistakes; they find it too embarrassing. In reality, Hunters learn very quickly from mistakes; they do a quick self-reflecting exercise in their own head, make mental notes, and do not dwell on them. They are not interested in going over it again for the sake of 'appearing to learn something'.

Hunters have 'gut feelings' and use them regularly. They make some very difficult decisions with apparent ease, which can seem cold and unemotional. Hunters can be surprisingly logical at times, even though their hearts are always in the right place, and this can be overridden when their gut thinks it is the right choice. They will not be able to explain every choice, they just know it is the right one.

All Hunters want to push their family into the world and get their children to stand on their own two feet as quickly as possible. They want them to succeed and not have to keep dragging them along. Hunters are the people who go on world trekking holidays with their family; having a 5-year-old child will not stop them doing the Inca trails, as they believe it will be a good life experience for them.

A Hunter wants to instil passion and independence into their children. They want them to be strong-willed, to stand up for themselves, pushing them from an early age to succeed. Hunters cannot wait for children to become more independent, because then they can start interacting with their children and have a little more time for themselves. Children, to a Hunter, should not be a reason to stop having fun, but instead they must become part of it.

In business, Hunters are incredible negotiators. They have a unique ability to communicate with anyone. Their open personalities and directness makes meetings fun and productive.

Hunters see opportunities to better themselves. They are willing to jump in with both feet. They may not ride the opportunity train all the way to the end station, as there may be a better one waiting for them at the next stop. They are, however, guaranteed to keep passengers entertained and enthralled throughout their journey. They are incredibly persuasive and can convince people using tales of experience and a show of knowledge.

Hunters are more 'performer' than 'spectator'. They have great pride and want to win because losing is embarrassing. They have no problem in embellishing a few facts just to make sure they are on the winning side of an argument.

Hunters hate detail and want to work with only brief sets of instructions. Hunters prefer to learn as they go, rather than rely on a 'recognised' learning process.

Once a Hunter thinks they have mastered a skill, they instantly want to teach it. They will want to demonstrate this expertise or start conversations to discuss this new understanding. Hunters do not like to look weak and will prefer to learn subjects by themselves. Giving them access to the internet and references will produce better results than being part of a group with a teacher.

Hunters want to be seen as an authority on everything that they get involved with. They will have put in a lot of hours, finding out what they need to know on the given subject. Hunters have a short attention span when it comes to instruction. They will always fail to read long and 'important' emails, and ignore user manuals. They only have to look at the length of the message to decide that they are not going to read it. If it is not immediately deleted, it probably will be after the first paragraph if it does not get to the point of the message.

Hunters often get into trouble for doing this, as they miss the small things in the message. If you have to send a long email to a Hunter, do not explain why you are sending it, get to the point; use bullet points and keep it short.

Hunters need quick, easy to understand and practicable instructions. They learn much faster with the actual doing of a task, than from any reading or classroom lecturing. They are the 'kinaesthetic' style learners.

Hunters do not like being wrong; even when they are presented with undisputable evidence, they will try and ignore it or worse, justify their reasoning. The fact that they are wrong will not change their opinion of their thought process. Even if they say otherwise, they still think they are right; they just want to move on and stop the ongoing embarrassment.

Hunters find it hard to apologise for mistakes, as it means prolonging the shame. They will apologise if this solves a problem and they know people can move on and not bring it up again.

All Hunters are true fighters and will fight for their position in the tribe. They cling to their morals and beliefs, and have no concerns about telling someone that they are wrong.

A Hunters needs variety, and problems arise when they get bored. They can easily dismiss the importance of a task if it is part of daily life. They do not like people who do not 'get' them; they stay with friends who understand them as they do not want to have to justify their actions all the time. They have very little time and will probably ignore people who they think are just being picky or who want to lecture them about life.

Hunters can be seen as being misleading, saying one thing and meaning another. This tends to happen when Hunters are still working things out for themselves. When they are asked for their thoughts, they will just blurt out their current thinking. Hunters are like the air; they have fluidity in their thoughts and are willing to change their minds at a drop of a hat if they think they can get a better outcome.

Hunters are the 'glass is half full' thinkers. Most of the time, Hunters are keen to get things started and will not have thought through the whole plan. Any changes that they make will come with their own reasoning. These might be flawed to someone else, but to a Hunter it makes perfect sense. No amount of complaining from others will get them to admit that they have made the wrong decision, not until the whole thing fails, and if it does, Hunters will still think it was a partial success.

If you want a Hunter to learn or to be productive in a meeting, don't use long PowerPoint presentations. If there are too many words and no pictures, they will have lost interest.

Hunters treat long distance e-learning packages the same way as PowerPoints. They know they need to be completed and will find a way to get to the end as quickly as possible. They will probably turn it into a competition, making speed, not learning the objective, showing off the time in which they completed the course.

Hunters like quick wins. They are happy to complete 20 short tasks in a day rather than one massive task over a week. A Hunter has a good attention span, but if something more interesting comes along, they refocus their energy away from the old task.

If a Hunter does lose focus, they need to be reminded of their original task. The easiest way to get a Hunter to start work again is to praise their efforts. Making them feel that they are the only person for this task, that only they are trusted to complete it to the expected high standard they are capable of, will bring their attention back. This is more than enough encouragement to get them moving again, and they will probably complete the task ahead of schedule.

Upsetting a Hunter and getting them to push their button is easy. If they feel restricted, they start to feel the stress. Stopping them from doing what they want to do, and how they want to do it, will lead to conflict. They will feel like they are being attacked and they will fight ferociously to do what they want, when they want, and the way they want it. If a Hunter is given a goal, it has to be simple, flexible and with little instruction included. The more simple a goal is, the more chance of it being completed.

Hunters need to be kept busy, but only with important tasks. Even if it is the most mundane task in the world, it has to be sold as the 'key' to the whole process; it is the most important job that needs doing and only they have been chosen to do it.

Expecting them to do 'nothing' is inviting trouble. If work is waiting to be done and a Hunter knows what is expected of them, let them get on with it. Micromanaging a Hunter, or giving a Hunter a little task in a larger project, will get them pushing their own buttons. They find ways to entertain themselves; in these situations, they can overstep their mandate, leading to them interfering in other people's work. Hunters can become preoccupied with whatever they find to do. If they believe they can plug a gap, they will work tirelessly to the point of distraction to do their bit.

Hunters handle short stressful situations extremely well; they stay calm and unflustered. Put a Hunter into a long-term stressful situation and expect them to lose their cool and get angry, because they do not see any result from their effort. If there is no end to a stressful situation, they will probably explode.

Hunters cannot bottle stress up like other tribe members. When they reach saturation point, they will not give any notice before they fly off the handle. They appear to cope right up to the point that they bite someone's head off. Whoever that person is, they will get the full release, whether they deserved it or not. Then it can get a bit messy, especially if it is the boss.

Once a Hunter has vented their frustration, they will instantly forget about the stress and return back to the task in hand. They seem to forget about everything that has just happened, and they will expect to pick things up again from where they left off.

Hunters will treat everyone the same, not necessarily as their equals but there are no presumptions until they know different. Hunters do not recognise people's personal boundaries and have no problem being 'over friendly' with people they have only just met. They think it is normal to call their doctor by their first name or think of their big boss as a 'mate'.

Hunters are quick to learn where someone's personal line has been drawn. By telling a Hunter what is comfortable and what isn't will change their response. Providing they are not belittled about it, they will conform; however, if people snap at them, it will become a game and they will continue to overstep the mark until they get bored or an apology.

Hunters are typically trusting characters. They are willing to see the good in people until they have seen, learnt or experienced a few harsh facts about them. Hunters do not take part in grudge matches; they just ignore people that they no longer want to interact with. They have long memories and if people cross a Hunter, they can expect never to receive a Christmas card again. If a Hunter has been wronged by someone, people will know it because they will refuse to speak or interact with them. This may seem a little childish but there is little anyone can do to change this decision, except when that person gives an apology and tries to make it up to the Hunter, otherwise it gets uncomfortable for lots of people.

Keeping a Hunter productive and getting them to use their natural abilities is an easy task. Setting a goal and asking them to complete it by playing a little to their ego helps. Add to the request by mentioning that they were the first person that came to mind for this job is a good start. By not setting firm guidelines and never going into detail about how it should be done, unless asked, is another good step. Telling them it is a challenge also whets their appetite.

When the result of the task is shown, no matter the outcome, their effort needs to be appreciated. Whatever they show as their finished product, even if it is not what was expected, heap on some praise and recognition of their achievement before you ask them to change or modify any of it.

Hunters do not like to be wrong and hate to be criticised when they are. If you need to speak to a Hunter about the quality of their work, do not do this in the office full of people. Take them for a coffee and get them relaxed. Try not to give feedback in a formal setting, such as across a desk. Hunters react better when they see the whole of a person, as they pick up on body language. Telling a Hunter they got it wrong over the phone or by email will not get a good result.

Hunters are proud individuals; they want to show off their achievements to anyone that asks and even to those who don't. If you upset a Hunter and push them over the edge, you will know it very quickly. When a Hunter feels threatened, they will push their button. They will be ferocious, fighting and arguing until they win or suffer from burnout.

If there is a need to give feedback to a Hunter, start by talking about positive achievements and then slip in some feedback. Asking them to say what they got wrong gets a better response than when it gets pointed out. Surprisingly, Hunters are good reflectors, so they have probably already gone through their own process and will have already worked out what they would do differently the next time. They do not need to discuss these things so once they have spoken about it, don't drag it out for any longer than it needs to be. Finish by adding a phrase to make them feel better, something along the lines that they are still a trusted individual and are recognised as a hard worker.

Only if a Hunter needs to be disciplined, should a formal meeting be considered, otherwise keep it light and friendly. You will both get much more out of it with these types of discussion.

~

TIPS FOR HUNTERS,
WHEN THEY DEAL WITH OTHERS.

Hunter vs Hunter

When a Hunter interacts with another Hunter, this will be a match made in heaven but only at the beginning. Both will feed off the other's enthusiasm and ideas. It will be an explosive combination, challenging each other constantly and enjoying the competition. They will feed off each other's support, coming up with their next crazy idea. They will have made a strong friendship, spending a lot of time with each other. Over a period of time, they will start to lose interest in the other, and one will start to sabotage the relationship. They will throw spanners into the relationship and will watch it crash and burn.

Hunters are great together if there is equilibrium, but when one Hunter appears to be more successful that the other, this is the beginning of the end. All the limelight will be on the stronger Hunter; they will be enjoying this attention and will expect the other to give some recognition. This leads to the underdog scenario, where the weaker Hunter no longer feels worthy and will go looking for someone who they can compete with.

If they feel they have to fight for some attention from the other, they find it easier to look elsewhere.

The stronger of the two Hunters will continue to enjoy being the top dog. They will carry on the friendship regardless as Hunters do not pick up on subtle hints. They do not see this from the other's point of view. When dynamics change in a Hunter pairing, it normally spells the end. Hunters do not like to show weakness or to speak about not being 'respected' by the other. Hunters expect attention but do not ask for it. They are loud and show off to get it, but they are one-trick ponies; if it no longer works, they will try it on someone else.

Hunter vs Protector

Hunters and Protectors can either be a perfect match or a fight waiting to happen. Hunters see Protectors as being too serious and they have no problem poking the 'hornet's nest' just to lighten the mood. Hunters will not understand why the Protector suddenly goes off on one, as it's only 'a joke'.

Normally the Hunter and Protector have a mutual respect for each other and will get along. Both appear to be dedicated and hard-working, which is important. Neither beat around the bush about delivering a bad message.

133

The Hunter's direct approach can seem comical to a Protector who is far more serious.

Problems arise when the Hunter finds something more enjoyable to do rather than the task set by a Protector. The Hunter will not be concerned about not completing a task and will justify their actions by saying that the new task is a better use of their time. Protectors do not see this as justification and believe the Hunter is just being lazy. Protectors have a set mind of completing one task before moving on, whereas the Hunter is happy to chop and change tasks.

A Hunter can learn a lot from a Protector; being a little more focused and dedicated in completing important tasks is a good beginning, and also finding better ways to communicate. Being able to explain their thought process quickly without going off on tangents will impress a Protector. If a Hunter needs to improve a relationship with a Protector, then they need to think a little more and consider being more serious around them. Taking responsibility and ownership of menial tasks without fighting or expecting any form of thanks will be a good start.

Hunter vs Gatherer

A Hunter and Gatherer pairing is like watching a game of Buckaroo. You know that the donkey is about to kick off, but you are not sure when. When the donkey finally kicks off, it will make everyone jump and spectators laugh. Hunters are free Air spirits and Gatherers are Earthy process-driven, fixated individuals. Gatherers do not understand the Hunters 'suck it and see' attitude. They would rather think about it, come up with a plan and do it once, not the 'jump in and have a go' scenario.

A Hunter believes that a rigid and fixed-minded Gatherer does not see the whole picture. A Gatherer will never see a problem the same as a Hunter. The fluidity and rigid natures of both means that any process either one comes up with will be rejected by the other. When a Hunter tries to explain a result to a Gatherer, the Hunter will talk about all the exciting and wonderful results that they feel were the best. A Gatherer does not do 'emotion', they only want the facts and how the results were arrived at. They will want to know that a process was followed, so if a process needs to be corrected, it can be changed at any stage the next time. Hunters do not understand this inability to be flexible, and friction is caused.

Hunters and Gatherers do not see eye to eye as they both think that their ways are best. They may start being 'nice' but there is only one way that this will go. Hunters expect Gatherers to see it their way.

Gatherers continually ask 'stupid' questions of the Hunter, as the Hunter sees them as obvious answers. Both will get more annoyed with each other as the relationship grows. Most interactions between this pair will result in the Hunter shouting and storming off with the Gatherer withdrawing from the task and refusing to co-operate with the Hunter again.

There is very little that can be done for these two. When the Buckaroo goes off, only the Hunter can reset it. If the Hunter is successful, they will both start to load the donkey again and the same sequence of events will happen.

Hunters who want to get the best result when working with a Gatherer have to learn to bite their tongues. For a successful pairing, they should not work in the same office. They need to limit contact with each other, in person and by email. Scheduling short, regular meetings with each other will appease both sides. The aim is to only put a few things on the donkey at any one time and not let the donkey kick off.

Hunter vs Healer

Hunters and Healers are both very open tribe members. They both enjoy talking and dealing with emotions. They get on particularly well with each other and will find themselves being good friends.

Hunters, when they become comfortable in a friendship with a Healer, will start to become more adventurous, which the Healer will not like but will go along with it. The direct nature of the Hunter means they are the ideas person, suggesting where to go and when to meet up. The Healer will go along with these suggestions but can start to withdraw. The Hunter needs to recognise this in a Healer as they will not mention it. Hunters can take over in these relationships so being more mindful will help. If the Hunter speaks to a new group, the Healer will need to be introduced to them all. The Healer will appreciate this and feel more secure in the friendship and that they are not being replaced.

Healers and Hunters make wonderful companions. The indirect nature of the Healer means the 'over the top' Hunter behaviour will not be challenged, it gets ignored. A Hunter needs to check how a Healer is feeling on a regular basis, which can seem a little much for a Hunter, but means the world to the Healer.

Spending some time alone together, discussing personal or business matters, will score highly for the Healer. There is nothing more endearing to a Healer than knowing some personal stuff about a Hunter. A Healer is actually in awe of a Hunter, and if a Hunter manages to remember certain things about the Healer, it will be a really good pairing.

WE CAN IMPROVE
OUR RELATIONSHIPS
WITH OTHERS
BY LEAPS AND BOUNDS
IF WE BECOME
ENCOURAGERS
INSTEAD OF CRITICS.

JOYCE MEYER

8. PROTECTORS

Get on with it.

Protectors have both Closed and Direct personality traits. Protectors are closest to the Fire element. Our Caveman ancestor Protectors will have known that they had a very important job but they wouldn't have gone on about it. They will have been big, tough and been able to defend the tribe from any outside threats or aggressors. Protectors will have been the ones who managed the tribe's rules, ensuring they were enforced and people got punished for breaking them. They will have followed these rules and agreements, getting very upset when people broke them.

Protectors will have been the disciplinarians of the tribe. Their job of protecting the cave and its occupants will have been seen as them being in charge of the tribe. They will have believed there is no time for fun as they had an important task to complete. They are selflessly working for everyone's benefit. They could enforce the rules and dish out any punishment for breaching security and most of the tribe feared them for their authoritarian outlook. They will have been 100% focused on the task of protecting the tribe.

If they felt that someone was purposefully exposing the tribe to unnecessary danger, they will take matters into their own hands. The Protector will first correct the wrong, fixing the problem, then they will deal with the person breaching the rule.

Protectors will have been big and strong, not only physically but mentally as well. They had a compass for right and wrong, and had an overriding drive to look after those that needed protecting. They defended their tribe, even when it had to be protected against its own stupidity.

Modern-day Protectors will not have changed much. They probably wear warmer clothes and have better teeth, but their feeling of responsibility has remained the same.

Protectors want to be in control, and therefore in charge. They do not necessarily want to be the top honcho, but they cannot tolerate someone who is in a powerful position and doing a bad job. They will want to take matters into their own hands and can be seen as being promotion ladder climbers, only wanting to right the wrongly appointed "buffoon's" decisions. It is the drive to do things right that pushes them, rather than a want to be at the top.

Protectors are the decision makers and the task masters of the tribe. They are the epitome of the saying, "Do what I say, not what I do." They are very pushy and incredibly stubborn when they believe that they are right, and that will be all the time. They want people to work hard; fun does not come into it as it delays the outcome and takes people's focus away from the task. People cannot ease off unless they are on top of all their work or if the task is drawing to an end. Once the job is complete, the Protector is happy to party as hard as they work; they can be intense people in or out of work.

Protectors are very practical and have strong personal values. They believe that people need a strong work ethic, and they demand that people and institutions take responsibility for their  actions. Protectors have fiery tempers and do not like it when people cannot understand the importance of following rules. They have little sympathy for people who break them as they believe individuals should accept the consequences if they decide to step outside of the guidelines.

Protectors do not like to be wrong. Actually, if you ask a Protector, they will tell you that they are never wrong! Protectors are control freaks. They do not like people messing with one of their rules. If the rules say that people need to follow a process, then people need to follow it, no shortcuts, just follow the rules. Even if someone tries to make something better or quicker, if it is outside the rules, a Protector will not like it.

Being a Protector means that they prefer the task to be completed the right way and if someone wants to mess around with doing it a new way, they can do it in their own time. If there is a schedule to follow, the rules mean people must prepare for it and then follow the timings. A Protector will even make sure others prepare and follow them as well.

Protectors prefer to be given tasks that have an end to them. They like to measure results, especially if it comes with a number. The measurements can be quantity, cost or anything that can use a number. Protectors like to complete tasks, show the result, notch up another count and then move on to the next task. They are results orientated and are happy to complete a new task immediately after finishing the last one. They like to keep tally and use this as proof of their abilities.

A Protector is an effective team worker; their focus is on the task. Their attitude towards guidelines and rules can make them appear to be bossy. They can be seen as patronising, uncaring and even aggressive when others try to do the same task outside of the approved technique. Protectors can be consumed by a task and be unaware of their dwindling communication skills as they become efficient rather than polite. Protectors can switch between conversations very quickly and can become upset when others lose the thread of the conversation.

Protectors can come across as know-it-alls. They spend hours learning how to do a job properly and they can become an authority on the subject. They are incredibly reliable and will not mince their words if they need to tell it 'how it is'.

Protectors are one of the more responsible people in the tribe. They have an air of authority and have a fiery temper if people try and cross them. Give them a task and allow them to get on with it; they will follow the rules and bring back a fast result.

Protectors believe in common sense and are conventional in sticking to traditional, acceptable behaviours and skills. They will try to preach these ways of working to those who do not conform. Protectors can be quite intense in their 'negotiations' and 'suggestions' but they do not like to argue.

Protectors are the first to challenge poor behaviour. They have high standards and they do not like people who are tardy or unprofessional. They are outspoken about these things and have no concerns about telling individuals that they have let the side down, embarrassing them in front of others. They want people to do what is expected of them, no more and no less.

If a Protector has a good manager, they will settle into their role and they are guaranteed to be a brilliant worker. If they believe that their boss is weak or not doing a good job, their focus changes and they will want to be in charge. They believe that they can do a better job and set their sights on working their way up the ladder, all through hard work and dedication.

Protectors do not like asking for help. When given an unfamiliar task, they will learn a role by seeking people they trust and they know are an authority on the subject matter, and they will master it and produce quality results. Although they can complete numerous, multiple tasks at once, they do not like to finish a task until they have completed everything that they believe they needed to do on it.

Protectors become the morality moderators when people step out of line. They try and mould people into how they think others should react in a given situation.

Protectors are so task orientated they do not like to waste their time. If a conversation is needed, make sure the point is made quickly and any pleasantries are forgotten. A quick hello is about the limit and this can sometimes be dispensed with.

Protectors have such a strong sense of duty and belonging, they cannot turn a blind eye to anything that they feel is not quite right. They want to be respected for what they are able to achieve and they need to get some form of recognition for their work. They are not concerned about big announcements, a personal thank you will do.

When giving credit to a Protector, it has to be for their genuine hard work and effort. If they detect any sarcasm or misgivings in the praise, they will feel devalued. Protectors will tackle the next challenge with or without a thanks. However, if praise is not given when they feel it is necessary, they will ask for feedback.

Most Protectors seek security and place their trust in authority, even if they know that those who are placed above them may be incompetent. They are loyal and steadfast to the management decisions; they believe in such things as rank, file and order.

They understand that management structure is there for a reason and they do not believe in undermining any manager. Protectors are loyal to their work, their family and their friends, and they will defend these institutions if they need to and will not stand for anyone disrespecting people they feel they owe something to.

Protectors are very adept at understanding rules. They know which ones need to be adhered to and they are aware of the ones where people may be allowed to stretch them. Protectors are quite practicable and understand that there is not the 'one rules that fits all'. If they need to, they can step outside of the rules, providing it is ethical and in the spirit of achieving a goal, they will be happy to support such actions.

Protectors like information, but not detail. They want things spelt out in bullet points, not in long, complicated, detailed reports. Protectors can pick up someone's viewpoint very quickly; they like people to be accurate and brief as this will not waste their time.

Protectors are quick visual learners; they watch and replicate what they see. They are fast learners, and if the pace of teaching is too slow, they will hit their button and get frustrated. They have little patience for slow learners as these people are stopping them from achieving their goal.

Protectors like to be efficient. If a meeting has been scheduled for a specific time, do not turn up late. If people are late, expect a dressing down or a sarcastic comment in front of the others in the room, regardless of any excuse.

A Protector provides stability within their family; they want a secure home and they will teach their children right from wrong. They can become comfortable in love and not feel the need to keep showing it.

'Emotion' is just a word to a Protector and it gets in the way of doing more important stuff. They develop deep relationships with their loved ones, but once things are settled, they do not see the point of having to remind someone that they love them. They need to be asked to show emotion; their feelings run deep and they can be hurt, but they will not show it in public.

A Stressed Protector is a criticising Protector. They become stressed when the rules are not followed or are unclear. They prefer to work in the 'black and white' of guidelines. They can operate in the grey areas around the edge of the rules, but they become less efficient and are more wary of making a decision.

Protectors like planning and are very quick at pulling a situation apart, understanding it and then giving a direction. They can always come up with a plan and once it has been formulated, they will follow it. They will only change their mind when it can be proven that another way is more efficient and a better use of resources.

If a Protector makes a mistake, do not worry about trying to soften the blow. Take them somewhere private and get to the point fast. Tell them where the mistake was made and be prepared to argue. Have some facts and evidence ready and once they have had a chance to digest the feedback, they will accept it, pass thanks and will be expected to be given the opportunity to go back and correct matters.

Upsetting a Protector is easy; break a promise or an agreement and watch them hit the button. Not doing something that was agreed is a deal-breaker. They use trust in most of their negotiations. If the trust has been abused, a Protector has a long memory and they will refer back to specific incidents to justify not having faith in someone. It takes months of effort by someone to prove their worthiness again, so it is easier not to upset a Protector in the first place.

If a Protector has been upset, leave them to their own thoughts and get out of their way. They will not explode but they do become angry and will snap if you get too close. Do not think they need their hands held or a shoulder to cry on; this will not help the situation. Once they have calmed down, they will seek out someone to talk to, but they will only confide in people they truly trust. Space and time is the best medicine when it comes to dealing with an upset Protector.

Protectors keep their focus on a task until it is complete. They will procrastinate over a task if they do not have time to finish it in one period. They will delay starting tasks if it means they have to stop at some point. They would much rather complete it in one go, than to take a break overnight and finish it tomorrow.

Protectors are control freaks and they like to be challenged by being given increasingly harder tasks. They see these complex assignments as a recognition and acknowledgement of their abilities.

Protectors do not hide their frustration well and can be seen as aggressive and fiery. People who do not know them well tend to stay away as Protectors 'frighten' them. Those that are used to this persona can see past the frustration. They know that there is no harm in these outbursts and that the Protector is just trying to get the job done.

Most people will like the protection that a Protector offers. Providing people work within the rules, they know that if they need someone to fight their corner, a Protector is the person to ask.

Protectors like to operate in areas that they are familiar with. If they are asked for a decision on an unknown subject, they will not hazard a guess. They prefer to be right and they can only be right if they know what they are talking about. They will ask to delay a response so they can find out the right reply or they will suggest alternative people to ask. They will not be drawn into making an on the spot comment as this might lead them to be wrong.

~

TIPS FOR PROTECTORS, WHEN THEY DEAL WITH OTHERS,

Protector vs Protector

Protectors are normally very good together. They have mutual respect for each other's integrity. They will support the other Protector unless they believe they are in some form of competition with them. Protectors want to be in charge, even if everyone in the group has the same grade. Protectors will not openly undermine each other, but they will rally support and surround themselves with people who will champion their cause, believing a larger support group will prove their dominance.

Protectors do not show emotion and in a relationship with another, they can seem cold and very business-like. The house will be well-run and organised. There is a mutual understanding between them that one does not need to explain why to the other. They do acknowledge the other's achievements, seeing it as more of a competition. Protectors will set a task to become friends with each other; they will schedule a meeting for a coffee, or a weekly squash game. As long as they do not talk about emotions, they will pencil something into their diary.

Protectors can learn a lot from another Protector, but only if they are both willing to concede some authority to the other. The only way they will do this is when there is a mutual respect and trust for each other. They find tasks like this hard, being control freaks; they have to rely now on others. They will, however, be more comfortable giving responsibility to another Protector as they have made sure they have similar standards and are following the rules.

Protector vs Gatherer

Protectors and Gatherers can have a good relationship as neither of them want to deal with emotions. Both are happy to deal with any given task and they do not need any idle chit-chat before they get into it. There is a mutual respect of following the rules from both sides. The direct approach of the Protector can make the Gatherer feel undervalued as they cannot communicate the same way to defend their actions.

Protectors and Gatherers do not worry about pleasantries, and the relationship is very business-like. Protectors tend to overrule the Gatherer. The Protector, being a control freak, gives out the tasks and a specific set of instructions. Gatherers like information, and the more information and justification a Protector can give, the more eager a Gatherer will be. A set procedure with a list of long instructions and a PowerPoint presentation is all the Gatherer wants before they get going. However, the Protector will see this as a waste of time, and frustration can happen when there is no progress.

The Protector will get upset with a Gatherer when they ask too many "What if..." questions. Protectors have a short fuse and can believe that there is too much talking and discussion going on and no action. They will blame the Gatherer, calling them problem makers, rather than spending a little longer with them. The Protector will not accept they have not given clear enough instructions as they do not understand that Gatherers need more time and more information than others. Protectors should not expect a Gatherer to complete a task quickly. If a Protector knows that they are going to meet with a Gatherer, they should put time into the preparation with lots of handouts. Email them so the Gatherer does not ponder on them in front of the Protector, and then things will move more quickly.

Protector vs Healer

Protectors and Healers are the complete opposite of each other, so they complement each other's traits. The flexible nature of the Healer means they are happy to go along with suggestions from a strong personality, such as the Protector. The Protector is an efficient task orientated machine, and a Healer will not want to cause upset, they only want to please. They hear the importance of the task in the stern tones of the Protector and need little convincing of which task is more important. The Protector needs to remember not to overwork a Healer, as they do not say no.

Protectors are not emotional, and Healers try and get them to open up as they want them to 'feel' better about things. Healers need to know what is going on under the tough exterior of a Protector and they will ask personal questions, Protectors see this as interfering, rather than helping; it gets annoying when someone asks "Are you alright?" all the time. A Protector is not interested in the dynamics of friendship when at work; they will share personal thoughts, but only if they have a genuine friendship with the Healer. If a friendship is no longer working, it will be the Protector who stops contact, and they let the relationship wilt. The Healer will ask what went wrong but the Protector will not get involved; they will probably ignore these questions, unless that Healer becomes useful again.

A Protector needs to be reminded of the kind nature of a Healer. If they want to improve their relationship with a Healer, they need to listen to some 'woe is me' stories and not be tempted to fix it for them with a short, snappy answer. A Protector may need to open up and give them one of their own personal stories, showing that they have trust in the Healer.

Protector vs Hunter

Protectors see Hunters as 'noise'. They can get along really well, but when there are issues, it will be because Hunters are seen to be jokers and not to be trusted with important tasks. At times, Hunters are just not serious enough for Protectors. They are both high performers and both get their work done, but Hunters do not stick to the rules and this frustrates the Protectors. They like plans and rules, but Hunters want things to be more fluid, which will drive a Protector wild as they see them 'flitting' between tasks.

Hunters can bring Protectors back to humanity, showing there is more to life than being task orientated. They can give a Protector a release from the daily drain of completing task after task. Protectors can only stand so much messing from a Hunter, and their short fuse can regularly be lit from all the 'messing around.' The fall out can be quite short as a Protector wants to get on with a task and it will be like water off a duck's back to a Hunter. They will both find common ground again and quickly get on with things.

The Protector will usually recognise the Hunter's emotions, as it will have been pushed down their throats by the Hunter. The Hunter is the only other tribe member who will tell a Protector how it is. This partnership will make a Protector more rounded and less sharp, as the feedback can be brutal but necessary. Hunters and Protectors make brilliant companions. Protectors will quickly recognise a Hunter's unorthodox approach and will credit them after good results. Hunters have skills and abilities that a Protector will use, especially the no fear aspect and the want to get on with a task. The main drawback is when a Protector does not make a big deal when a Hunter is proud of a result.

I'VE LEARNED THAT
PEOPLE WILL FORGET
WHAT YOU SAID.
PEOPLE WILL FORGET
WHAT YOU DID.
BUT PEOPLE WILL
NEVER FORGET HOW YOU
MADE THEM FEEL.

MAYA ANGELOU

9. GATHERERS

Tell me more and don't spare any of the details.

Gathers are both Closed and Indirect. They are the closest tribe member to the Earth element. Our ancestral Cavemen Gatherers were the cautious ones of the group. They would be suspicious of everything and everyone, whether they knew them or they had only just met. They would not have put themselves in harm's way, unless they carried out some sort of risk assessment first. They were the first to have thought of something like our 'Health and Safety', and probably went around training people on how to handle fire before they were allowed to discover it.

They were the sensible ones of the tribe, standing back, watching people fail, taking notes of how not to hurt themselves and not ending up on 'CaveTube fails'. They were the members who were making the plans of how to do it properly and telling others of their mistakes.

Cavemen Gatherers would have had their days planned, from what time to get up, where they were going and what they were going to eat. They made sure that everything on their to-do list was done before they got an early night.

They were the first ones to have worked out where the best sleeping positions were and they would have tried out several places to make sure it was. They would not have been the first ones out of the cave each day, but probably the second or third. They enjoyed the same routines, the same monotonous lifestyle. They did not like change. They were happy they knew what they were doing and did it again and again, day after day.

The Gatherers were the ones who kept the tribe ticking over; all the menial, boring tasks got done, collecting water, wood, berries. Gatherers would have just got on with it; there would be little complaining and their actions would have gone unnoticed. They did not need praising as the completion of the task, doing it the right way, was all that was required as the reward.

They would have been the ones who want the tribe to be an efficient place to live. Gatherers would be planning for the future, making rules and policies, and then making sure everyone knew them. They could have been seen as busybodies; however, people appreciated their input once they had calmed down.

Gatherers had a trust issue. They only trusted themselves and those who had proved themselves as loyal and worthy.

Gatherers were happy to be loners. They would leave the cave to go foraging by themselves and would not need the interaction of a team. They knew what they were looking for and did not need someone interfering in their work. They would be looking for their tried and tested foods, and would not want to try new berries, plants or other things that they could eat.

Gatherers would bring back just enough food for the tribe to eat and be satisfied with. They did not see the need to bring as much food as they could, as they understood such things as waste. Their careful planning would dictate how much they should get and their plans included exactly how many berries they needed. They would not want to waste any of their hard work of gathering if it did not benefit the tribe.

Gatherers were forward planners. They would have started collecting sticks and bits of wood, thinking these items might be handy if the tribe were to invent something like fire. This was the kind of eventuality Gatherers would have been planning for. They were the "Yes, but..." members of the tribe, always trying to cover every angle.

Modern-day Gatherers still have the same traits, yet now there is less of an overbite, and they will have an iPad or tablet with a 'To Do' app on display. They will be checking results and recording things as they go about their daily chores, which must have purpose and must be worth their time.

Gatherers love a good process. They are the happiest when they follow a pre-planned process that will deliver the same result time after time. They do not like change so a process needs to be followed, to the letter with no deviation. The more information they can gather about the process, the more comfortable they will be with the task.

As Gatherers like to keep their feet on the ground, they are the 'salt of the Earth' types. Providing they are given enough information, they are happy to continue with things. This chapter is purposefully a bit  longer for that very reason. If a Gatherer gets enough information from this book, they will be more comfortable with the Caveman Principles, and the CTS. They need to be provided with this extra information, cover more examples of it working, and repeating certain scenarios for them to appreciate the benefits.

I might even slide in a PowerPoint or two, just for them to watch at their leisure on my website: www.carlrosierjones.com.

Gatherers need to collect as much information as they can. They want all avenues, roads, footpaths, bridle ways, shortcuts and tunnels covered. They are the "What if..." crowd.

Their drive is to be so well informed, that they will have enough information to make an informed choice. They do not do gut instinct and dislike being forced into making decisions. They need to be allowed enough time to make these decisions, otherwise they will push their own button and refuse to give a response. They do not like to make mistakes. Gatherers need time to digest and assess all the information they have gathered and when they delay giving an opinion for this reason, they are seen as being 'difficult'. When a quick or simple decision is needed, people can get very irate with Gatherers; they can be said to have 'no backbone' as they are not willing to take any form of risk or a gamble. They take hours or even days to decide the best course of action, but this is how they operate; slow, methodical and rational. They need time to come to the right decision, or they get stressed and withdraw.

When Gatherers are allowed the time to make an informed decision, they are steadfast in their final judgment. They will have put a lot of work into the task and would have covered all eventualities. If their decision is challenged, they will have put so much data together to prove their theory, that most people's questions will have already been thought of and a reply will be waiting.

When a Gatherer gives information, they are the ones who state, "Tell them what you are going to tell them, tell them and then tell them what you have told them." This style of delivering information is widely accepted as the 'briefing model' but Gatherers love it and use it as often as they can. Gatherers are indirect when it comes to them needing to be forthright, unless there is a process that they can hide behind. They struggle to get straight to the point and will build up a conversation before they deliver their message.

Gatherers have a wealth of knowledge on a given subject and enjoy sharing it. If they believe that someone is doing a process wrong, they get quite irate about it. They can become vocal as they worry about the result. Instead of challenging the behaviour, they start to throw rules, laws and regulations at people, expecting them to know they have done something wrong and will change their ways because of this new information.

Gatherers do not like change but they love new technology. They can see it being worthy of their effort to learn about a new gadget if it is going save them time and effort. Gatherers learn best through reading and writing. They will research something new, find everything out about it, and then explore the best option of where to buy it. Price is just one factor, as a Gatherer will also look at the best guarantee, service cover and customer feedback. Once they have chosen where to get their new piece of kit, which can take some time, they will schedule it into their diary.

Unlike other tribe members, when they get their new toy home, the first thing to come out of the box will be the instruction manual. It will be read cover to cover before taking the gadget out of the box. This will be done for the most complex of toys, as well as for a toaster or a kettle.

For Gatherers, there is always something new to learn. They get comfort from pages and pages of information, even if most will believe it is not relevant. They have an ability to consume all data and store it for future use.

Gatherers learn best from reading, and even though they gain a firm grasp of the facts, they still then like to ask question after question to confirm their understanding.

Gatherers do not understand why people wouldn't want to sit through five hours of PowerPoint presentations for one training session. They love the fact that they can visualise the words on the screen as well as being told them.

If one person were to ask a question at the end of a training session, then you can put money on it being a Gatherer. A Gatherer's question can be identified by their natural call as it always starts with, "What if…." or "Just to clarify…" They cannot remain silent when given the opportunity to ask a question; they see it as a chance to clarify any ambiguities. They also enjoy staying behind to speak with the trainer at the end or a session, to try and glean any extra information or knowledge from them.

Gatherers learn so much faster if a process is taught through a structured plan. Gatherers do not do so well when a lot of information is thrown at them. They take loads of notes at meetings and will always have pages of references from any trainings they are given. It is necessary for them to take it all away so they can work through it all at their own pace.

Gatherers are naturally gifted strategists. Shops like the 'Games Workshop' where Warhammer and other games are played will be full of young Gatherers. These types of strategy based games allow the player to think about the next five steps. The game allows sufficient time to make reasoned choices and give the player time to assess each move. Gatherers also enjoy games like chess and Monopoly, dragging a game out for hours as they think about their next move.

Gatherers tend to stand out from a main bulk of the tribe as they can be seen as being a little bit different. This is partly because they chose not to mix with the rest of the tribe. Gatherers prefer the company of other Gatherers. They do not need social interaction from just anyone, and would prefer being alone rather than having to put up with someone who does not think the same way as them.

Gatherers are, by their own nature, knowledge seekers; they trust information, proven facts and trusted sources. They do not understand or accept the notion of a gut feeling, especially when important decisions are being made. They rely on their logical thought process, following what is in their head, and not in their heart. If a decision cannot be proven that it will work, or that it is the right choice for the group, then Gatherers will simply dismiss it.

When a Gatherer learns a new process, they will experiment with it until they trust it fully. When they have proven that it will work, they will use it time and again. They will even try to use the same process in other ways, if they think they are enhancing their status. Just read a Gatherer's email signature block; it will be long, full of information giving many different ways to contact them (rather than just pushing the reply button), and you can watch it growing in length and size over time.

They enjoy processes and are resistant to new ideas as they dislike change. Change needs to be assessed first as they do not use unproven theories. Everything about the new process will be carefully assessed and experimented on before they accept it.

As Gatherers like to follow a process, they can be seen as unyielding, refusing to deviate from the original plan. They will try and make a scenario fit a tried and tested process, rather than making a new process to fit the new scenario. They can get mixed results, but they also know where the process needs to be monitored and modified. Others will criticise their efforts, purely because they do not understand that a Gatherer needs to follow a process. They will change and modify it, but it can be a slow progression.

Gatherers are the 'belt and braces' kind of people. They exceed certain requirements when they complete any task. They would rather give a page justifying a response, rather than a simple one-word answer such as "Yes." Simple tasks like going to the cinema can take hours of planning.

They will check all the timings, what time it starts and when it ends. They will check where the best seats are in the theatre, what cinema has the best deal and how they are going to get there. If they manage to stick to their schedule, they will have a wonderful time. However, if there are any delays or people are late, they will be pushing their button. When a Gatherer finds a 'new' process and they have proven that it works, they will slot it into their daily tasks. They will use it whenever they can, if they believe it will benefit them. Gatherers have even been known to bolt on a useful process at the end of other processes, such as double bagging their shopping even if they have only bought a loaf of bread. These double and even triple-checked processes will mean that whatever they do, any mistakes are minimised, even if some of their intentions are unnecessary.

The concept of Health and Safety must have been championed by a bunch of Gatherers. It makes perfect sense that process driven individuals believe that going into minute details about how to operate any machine, tool or environment will reduce accidents. A little fact that Gatherers will feel proud of is that due to the efforts of people being able to cover all aspects of dangerous situations and since the introduction of Health and Safety legislation, the number of deaths and serious injury has been reduced dramatically.

Gatherers like writing really long, detailed emails. They have a big signature block at the bottom with loads of information, most of it being copied and pasted from somewhere. They do expect that the entire message will be read, as they have spent a lot of time preparing it for the recipients. Gatherers do not get to the point, and they hide the information they want to deliver in lots of text. The recipient has to read every line to understand the content and the clever Gatherer will have placed reasoned arguments either side of this information, justifying their decision and reducing people's misunderstanding.

Gatherers are meticulous which explains why they have to learn every process before they give it a go. If the process is long and convoluted, they excel at getting it right the first time. They might not be the fastest at completing a task, but their understanding of each step before they jump in will mean that they bring consistent results, and due to their knowledge, they will become the ideal trainer, if the process ever needs to be taught to someone.

Gatherers are determined. They rely on fact; facts and hard evidence can never be wrong! Once a Gatherer has made up their mind, they are strong-willed and it becomes very difficult to convince them to change it. They have gone through a mental process, weighing up odds, seeing different outcomes and settling on the perfect process.

Gatherers are indirect. They want things to be right all the time, and as they cannot trust other non-Gatherers to follow the right process, they often prefer to complete tasks themselves. Due to them not getting to the point quickly, they can get frustrated and be seen as rude when they realise someone has not done a 'prescribed' action properly. They cannot turn a blind eye to these actions and they push their button. They end up trying to correct people by shouting policy and 'accepted' standards at them.

If a Gatherer believes that a specific process is not being followed, they have to interfere and put it right. They don't worry about hurting someone's feelings if a process needs correcting, and they can take over the whole task to ensure it gets done right.

Gatherers can get so focused on a process that they can forget they are dealing with individuals. They do not mean to be rude, they are just task focused instead of being people focused. Gatherers apply themselves to learning and then teaching. Even if the person with whom they are teaching does not want their input, they will still preach the right way to do it as they feel a moral obligation to make sure it is done right.

Gatherers believe that they gain more authority and promotion at work through being an area specialist or based on their performance statistics. This is why they become obsessed with one area of work or are always recording their achievements.

Gatherers enjoy having complete control of a task, especially when they are the only ones involved. They are more relaxed when they are on their own, rather than being part of a team. As they have a trust issue in other people's abilities, they find it hard to believe that other people's work is up to their own standard. They feel uncomfortable when they cannot be certain that a process is followed properly. For this reason, a Gatherer will micromanage a task. They constantly need feedback and check that a process is being followed correctly, wanting updates and a progression report. They offer 'helpful' advice as they just want the job completed correctly.

Gatherers need time to complete any task as they do not function properly, pushing their buttons when asked to do a 'rush' job. They need exact figures and do not like it when people use 'best guesstimates'. If they are handed a completed portfolio and they believe part of it is based on best estimates, they will double-check figures and facts, needing to be fully satisfied that the conclusion was actually right.

Gatherers are great process managers. They do not get involved in emotion and are perfect for managing a factory production line. They expect everyone to conform to the same 'acceptable standard' and these standards are rigorously checked. They do get annoyed when people bring person issues into the workplace. They find it hard to associate why people's problems at home can't just stay there.

Gatherers do struggle to understand that they cannot control everything. As emotions cannot be controlled, they will probably shy away from anything that is connected with a sensitive matter.

Gatherers do not tend to go to social gatherings. They do not see the benefit of going out in their personal time to mix with people who they can chat to in the office. Unless there is a personal benefit of going to a social meeting, such as a chance to speak to their manager at a barbecue or a just a free lunch, they would prefer to stay away.

Gatherers are good at weighing up probabilities and looking for logical outcomes. They enjoy finding mistakes or errors, and feel it is their role to highlight these to others. To try and understand how a Gatherer thinks, imagine seeing 'time' as a sequence of many events all categorised and filed away in a logical order, rather than a smooth flowing timeline full of experiences, and you may start to understand how they operate.

Gatherers believe they are always right because they follow a system. They appear amazingly calm when others are in stressful situations, to the point where they appear not to be grasping the full set of circumstances. This non-show of emotion gives the Gatherer a bad reputation for not understanding the seriousness of an event, but actually what they are doing is putting all their effort and concentration into finding a resolve.

The only time a Gatherer loses their cool is when they are lost, with no information, no process to follow, and not knowing where they can turn for help. There are no emotions being shown; they just appear to tread water, getting anxious whilst they plan their next move.

If a Gatherer is pushed for an immediate decision, they will panic, hitting their stress buttons. They try to delay the answer, trying to give them time to think; they find excuses or ask numerous questions for the same reason. They will even need to go somewhere right at that point, so they can get away for some thinking time; they have to ponder all the possible outcomes.

Gatherers do get angry, but they rarely show it. If they lose their cool and start to shout, they show their frustration at the situation and not normally at the person. A Gatherer shouting is a rare occurrence; they prefer to talk at people instead. They bombard them with logical fact weaving in a point they are trying to make.

A Gatherer does not settle old scores; they make mental records of the wrongs carried out against them, only to use later if needed. They would rather stop interactions with someone and ignore them than carry on with the mistrust they feel. By withdrawing from a task and refusing to co-operate with people who have offended them, they feel that they are proving a point. They want to see that their withdrawer from a task will prove that it will fail without their knowledge and expertise input. They may even attempt to sabotage it, throwing in a few spanners and a little discord amongst the remaining team members.

Gatherers respond really well when they are asked for advice, especially if they are referred to as specialists, or because they have recognition as having experience in a specific area.

A Gatherer's written report will be long and it will contain lots of big, important 'buzz' words. Gatherers report writing skills ask, "Why restrict yourself to only five words when 50 conveys a point much better?" The bigger and more complex the word, the more a Gatherer feels it worthy to be used. They can write complex reports and fill it full of fact, giving reasons as to why they are making it so complex and full of fact.

Gatherers look after their family; they can push people into becoming self-reliant. They teach fact and reason, making their parenting skills a process, rather than an emotional and 'confusing' time for themselves and their children.

When they start a conversation, expect it to be about a process. They will bring up fact to justify their reason and they expect to be allowed to go on about it for a very long time. They get excited about detail and choose an audience that will appreciate their knowledge.

Gatherers cannot say no to extra work. They take on more tasks than they can handle, believing they are the only ones who can do it. When giving a Gatherer a task, it has to have a specific outcome. They do not like things that can change. They want to stick to the agreed pending result and not like it when people try and change the desired outcome. A Gatherer will scrap the whole project preferring to restart the whole process from scratch, rather than modify only part of it.

Gatherers are good at repressing their emotions. A stressed Gatherer can continue to work on a given task, but they start to become more demanding on others. They are not aware of this impact, as they believe they are just completing their work. When a Gatherer is stressed, they are intolerant of other people's 'stupidity'.

When a Gatherer needs to be challenged for under-performing, they will need lots of information, facts and figures before they accept it. They will need it to be spelt out in a logical and chronological order. Only after they accept the findings, will they need to be shown where they went wrong and will want some help to amend a broken process. They will, however, quickly adapt and move on.

Criticising a Gatherer in an open environment where others can hear, is not a good plan; they need a confidential environment. Do not shout at a Gatherer; forcing too many changes on them will get them to push their button. Patience and understanding is the key to get a Gatherer to change.

TIPS FOR GATHERER, FOR WHEN THEY DEAL WITH OTHERS.

Gatherer vs Gatherer

Gatherers have a healthy respect for each other. They both understand the importance of needing to discuss a process before starting any task. They make plans and will discuss many different ways of how to approach the task. Once they have agreed the correct process that they will follow, only then will they be happy to get on with it. As this type of planning takes time, along with their meticulous eye for detail, scheduling for completion will be longer than most. However, it is almost a guarantee that they will deliver on time, on budget, and will be happy to give plenty of progress reports.

Gatherers are quite status orientated. If they both believe that they are the more experienced of the two Gatherers, it will cause problems. They will not be able to discuss this matter with each other, as neither will be forthright in their views. They expect the other to acknowledge this status without the need to be outspoken about it. Problems can happen when one has already processed a plan, then the other wants to change part of it.

There won't be a fight, however. They will both talk 'at' each other, convincing the other that they are superior.

If two Gatherers go for a promotion, they become underhanded by recording each other's failures with evidence of poor decision making. They use it to show why the other does not deserve promotion, rather than demonstrating their own skills.

If Gatherers fall out with each other, it will be because of their status. They ignore and make snide remarks at each other. The quickest way to get Gatherers over a funk with each other is to mediate between them.

Gatherer vs Healer

Gatherers and Healers are both Indirect. Neither will push each other around, and both will probably be quite respectful of each other. The Gatherer will see a Healer as someone who is 'away with the fairies' all the time. Healers will be viewed as not being focused on the task; they trust their emotions and gut feelings too much, rather than trusting a carefully planned process that a Gatherer sees as being more useful. Healers tend to support Gatherers as they do not like upsetting people and they would rather give leeway than have to fight about who holds the higher status.

181

Gatherers not being open people will be uncomfortable about sharing their thoughts and feelings. This constant request to do so from a Healer will upset the Gatherer. The Gatherer will call this a distraction rather than open up and be honest about things. The Healer will see this as someone needing to open up and will keep on trying. Gatherers can ignore a Healer and even avoid them so they do not need to be asked to open up. The Healer will have their feelings hurt after having their efforts snubbed, and the Gatherer will feel uncomfortable for quite some time afterwards.

If a Gatherer needs to improve a relationship with a Healer, they will have to open up, becoming more of a friend. A Healer cannot ignore someone who is so insular and by sharing some personal thoughts with them, it will go a long way. Healers do not like lots of information, but they will listen if they feel that a Gatherer is showing some emotion with it. A Gatherer needs to learn to say thank you and "I feel..." a lot to a Healer and to be mindful, as they can take Healers for granted because they are so amenable.

Gatherer vs Hunter

Gatherers are so focused on their process that having a lively Hunter around can get them to press their button within seconds. It is likely that these two personalities can come to blows. When a Gatherer pushes their button, they start to shout at the Hunter, trying to get them to stop talking and focus. Hunters will see this as a game and start by winding up the Gatherer. After a while, the Gatherer ignores them and then the Hunter starts to get angry. Hunters will be the first to lose their temper; they will want to have an open and frank discussion with the Gatherer, but the Gatherer will no longer be interested, as they had their chance.

A Gatherer can use a Hunter's productive attitude and gain really good results. The coupling of the two can be an awesome mix; the speed of the Hunter with the feedback and communication of the Gatherer can impress many people. The plan will be to keep them separate, but if the Hunter has no idea of what a Gatherer is doing, then this can cause problems. If a Gatherer can separate a task into the thinking and doing side, and not stray into the Hunter's territory, then they can both work peacefully together. Hunters despise being micromanaged; however, Gatherers find comfort in knowing every step is being taken. A Hunter's work should not be inspected by a Gatherer in front of them as there will be criticism and the Hunter will not tolerate it.

If a Gatherer needs to improve a relationship with a Hunter, take them out for a beer. Meet them socially. This will show effort and willingness, which the Hunter will respect.

A Hunter needs to feel connected to people so they communicate with them. When things get too much for a Gatherer, they only need to say that they have a meeting coming up and need to prepare a PowerPoint presentation. The Hunter will not ask any questions and the Gatherer will be free to leave.

Gatherer vs Protector

Interactions between Gatherers and Protectors are usually quite good. They both like quantifiable results and focus on getting it right the first time. A Gatherer would rather take their time at the beginning to get things in place, whereas a Protector has little time to waste on discussing the best option and will want to get on with it whilst they assess the progress as they go. Gatherers like Protectors because they do not like emotions to get in the way of a task. The pair can become completely task orientated and complete their tasks to a high standard.

Gatherers do not get on with pushy Protectors; the ones who put short deadlines on tasks can really push their buttons. A Gatherer who needs to face a Protector will not be able to stand up for themselves. They prefer to not have confrontational conversations, as Protectors can be quite short. A Gatherer is not as adept at handling strong-willed

Protectors, and can easily be beaten into submission. The Protectors more dominant, direct nature can win every time. Instead, a Gatherer will start to withdraw and pass the task on to someone else.

If a Gatherer needs to improve a relationship with a Protector, they need to learn to stand up for themselves. Becoming a more forthright individual will catch the Protectors attention and it will start to show the Protector that the Gatherer is capable of making quick decisions. Being more direct about what they want is going to be uncomfortable, but this is the only way they will gain more recognition and a better relationship to prove they are worthy. Showing the Protector that they have some 'Grrrrrr' in them is the key. Earning the respect of a Protector takes time and perseverance, but as soon as change starts to happen, it will take hold quite quickly.

10. HEALERS
How are you feeling?

Healers are both Open and Indirect. They have the closest traits associated to the Water element. Our ancestral Caveman Healers would have been the ones who looked after the tribe. They would be caring for the sick and treating the wounded. They liked to be around people and especially around those who needed them. The tribe accepted the role of a Healer as the go-to person when someone needed someone to listen or just a little TLC. The Healer just wanted everyone to be healthy and happy. Healers were the 'people' pleasers of the tribe. Healers were the ones that the people in the tribe turned to when they wanted someone to listen. They were the ones the others offloaded their worries to. Healers were the gentle, kind and approachable individuals within the group. Undoubtedly, their caring attitude would have been taken advantage off by a few of the other tribe members. They would have been easy targets for the practical jokers and may have been easily swindled by a few as well.

Healers generally have the 'nice guy' outlook of life. It came from their openness towards others and combined with their indirect communication style, it meant they would not have wanted to upset anyone. They made brilliant Tribal teachers or were considered wonderful mentors. Their willingness to help others would have been used to help teach children how to fight, protect, gather or heal.

Healers would have been knowledgeable as they would have made an effort to understand the principles of the other trades of the tribe. They may have lacked the desire to do many of the tasks the others performed but they were capable of teaching and passing this basic understanding on to those who wished to learn. They would have been the ones trusted to speak or bless the luck of a hunt or similar ceremonies that a clergy would perform today. Their unbiased outlook of not wanting to take sides would have been used widely as the tribal mediator or as negotiator between tribes.

Most modern-day Healers can walk upright and they can operate a Breville sandwich toaster, but are still none the wiser to have worked out how not to burn their mouth on the melted cheese. Healers look for friendship and are often found sat on a fence when it comes to taking sides in an argument.

They are open and quite sociable. They are the ones who look after the group, especially the stragglers or the quiet ones. It is always a good plan to take a few Healers on a pub crawl as it guarantees people get home in one piece. Healers love to be part of a group and to chat about anything. They enjoy listening to others and just being part of 'something' bigger than they have when they are alone.

Healers like to look for problems. They try and read situations so they can make sure people are happy and are having a good time. They are the first to ask "Are you OK?" Their drive is to ensure people are looked after and cared for.

Healers become wonderful friends to many people. They are great counsellors as they love to hear about other people's troubles. They are always willing to give helpful, kind support to anyone that needs it. They are like the Water element of washing away troubles and always  being calm in their appearance when they help. A Healer will always be available to go for a pint; they will drop whatever they are doing to meet up, especially if someone says they need their help. They are the person that people call when they are feeling down or when things are not going to plan. Healers are trustworthy and are not interested in spreading gossip; they are excellent secret keepers.

Healers are interested in personal growth and are often found reinventing themselves, sporting new hairstyles and clothes, or finding new venues to visit. They enjoy social occasions and will always be the first to respond to an invitation.

Healers test themselves, wanting to be a better friend. They are the most sensitive person in the group and they will pick up if anyone is being negative towards them. They will change their own behaviour to become a more likeable person in a group, even if it is against their beliefs. They strive to make other people's lives better, as they believe that everyone deserves to be happy, even if they have to become a little upset when they help someone. They are imaginative thinkers and can be found daydreaming with all sorts of wonderful, lovely thoughts going through their minds. This is how they release their tension.

Healers are interested in health and psychology, learning new ways that they can help others. Their desire is to be seen as kind and helpful, which pushes them on to a more 'spiritual' path. This is a real boost to their caring image, but others in the tribe can see them as being a bit too 'hippy'. Healers do not like bad news; they will always be the first to reply on a negative Facebook status with "What's up, mate?" and they genuinely want to know if they can help or offer advice.

Healers have big hearts and believe that the world is essentially a good place to live. Bad people are seen as having good souls but having made a few bad choices. When a Healer sees suffering in the world, they feel the pain. They like to do things that help, volunteering or caring for a cause. They push different charities agendas, can collect money by sitting in a bath full of beans or joining in foolish adventures, all for it being a good cause. Healers can be found stood in public places, outside supermarkets, holding charity boxes and tins, or chasing people around the office to sign their latest sponsorship forms.

Healers take a holistic view of negative events; they believe in 'cause and effect'. They want to solve the world's hunger problems, give water to Africa, and treat every disease by raising money for them. They will plant rhubarb in their garden, and go over the top when it comes to recycling, in their attempt to save the planet.

Healers do not like to take sides as they want to be everyone's friend. This can upset some friends, as they believe that a Healer should only be loyal to them. Healers want high regard for them remaining unbiased. They want to be seen as the only person who can speak to both sides and be the mediator in most situations.

They are everyone's friend and will not want to be seen as taking sides, unless it is them who has been wronged.

Healers have deep emotions and they are very fragile. Healers can easily be hurt if they are accused of being nasty or uncaring. Healers view emotions like riding a roller coaster; they are always going up and down, but this is where they find their true friends. They are very quick to pick up on other people's emotions and will match them with their own feelings, so they are able to bond with people so much quicker. They trust their intuition and their gut instinct. Most of the time, they are 'bang on the money' and get it right. They like to be right, as it saves upsetting people when they have to apologise. A Healer's apology is always long, heartfelt and genuine.

Healers look for deep, meaningful relationships and when they look for a partner or even a friend, they want someone who they can connect with for many years. When they find their soulmate, they will lavish attention and love on them like no other member of the tribe can. They can seem stifling at times, but this just means that they have found someone they are prepared to spend a lot of time with, and they can go overboard with fuss and attention.

Healers see everyone as equals, and therefore have problems with authoritative figures. They get so involved with their emotions, they can come across as being impulsive, but having their heart in the right place.

Parent Healers are the most caring and loving of all the tribe members; they only want what is best for their offspring. They believe that being nice will teach their children ethics, and they themselves will become more caring. A Healer does not want to chastise their child, but instead they encourage them to find their own personality by trying new things. When their child has done something wrong, they would rather talk about feelings being hurt and trust issues, rather than shout and scream. They will also play for hours with their children. They can often be found engrossed in imaginative play, building a den, a tree house or fighting dragons to get out of the castle.

Healers need to be in a positive work environment. They can be the source of positive energy, always looking to cheer people up and to explain that things are not as bad as they seem. They act as counsellors to their team, a source of human understandings, the one who others go to when they feel bad about something; they are the trouble soothers.

They take responsibility for being the office social organiser, inviting people for end of week drinks and even putting on a summer barbecue.

As their name alludes, Healers can be found in abundance in any caring profession. The hospitals are full of them, not filling beds but running around looking after the sick and unwell. They thrive on helping people, so where humanity is required, you can find a Healer.

Healers love to learn. They are always open to new methods of doing an old process, and will even become excited in the thought that they will become better at their job. Healers are auditory learners; they like to talk about a new process and discuss the new ways of working. They learn through communication and open discussions with those involved in the training. Healers love to hear examples and talk about experiences people have had whilst finding these new ways of working. They are fascinated to find out why it works and to discuss how they can include it at the next available opportunity.

Healers are such kind souls that they can be taken advantage of by stronger characters. When they realise that their actions are part of a big conspiracy against them, they will get very hurt, and they will push their buttons and get very wound up. They dislike people who do not care. They will probably not shout at anyone, but instead they will withdraw from them and others, becoming a hermit for a while.

Healers put so much effort into helping others, they believe that others should do the same for them. They like to play out 'dramas' as a test on their friends. When people ignore their 'life-ending tragedy', Healers can get incredibly upset. All they want is some attention and affection from the people they have been looking after. It is a short-lived experiment by them testing their friendships so that they are not carrying all the emotional burden of the group and others can be relied on.

If you want to find the Healer in a group or just want to make them panic, throw an emotional hand grenade into the gathering by declaring that you dislike someone. Sit back and watch them calm everyone down. Pushing a Healer to take sides in an argument will also trigger a similar response as they make sure everyone is alright with their choice. If not, they will wriggle out of giving a decision.

Healers do not like people shouting. If a Healer needs to be spoken to about their performance, it should not be done publicly as this humiliates them because they are unable to respond when people shout.

Speaking to them in private and giving constructive feedback whilst adding lots of "we" into the conversation, such as "We feel that.." works so much better.

If a Healer does become upset, they will start to apologise a lot, saying that they are sorry for all sorts of things, whilst they attempt not to lose their patience. They do not show anger or retaliate like others in the tribe. They bottle up all their stress and will suddenly cut contact for a while. Once they have calmed down, they will reinitiate the relationship, but this cannot be hurried. Even if they are upset with just one person, they will not ignore them in case that same person suddenly needs the Healer's help.

Healers do their best work when they are allowed to use a combination of imagination, feelings and intuition. They produce some really good results, but they may not be able to explain how they managed to get this outcome as they will have difficultly quantifying their actions.

Healers are proud individuals and they feel insulted when someone does not show respect for their work or ask too many questions, appearing to pick at the decision. They cannot explain their intuition and gut feelings, either before, during or after the task. If praise is not offered or someone attempts to steal the limelight, it will lead to a Healer to feel undervalued and belittled with them not giving their all on the next task.

Healers work best when they are asked to use their skills and they see an opportunity to boost morale. They see themselves as people who can remove problems from others, allowing them to get on with their work and not be held back by their emotions. They ask people for an opinion and they take time to listen to their reply, making notes and making people feel valued in their team. If a Healer feels 'comfortable', they will put their entire soul into a project. They like to feel that something is worth their effort and they like acknowledgment from people enjoying the task.

To connect with a Healer is easy. They enjoy human contact, such as handshakes, so even greeting them with a hug will get them on board straight away. When they talk to people, they will reach out to touch them, either holding their shoulder or arm as they introduce an idea. Touching is the quickest way Healers link with others but they know the law and should stop before they get too far.

Healers try to keep eye contact with the person they are engaging conversation with. This shows them that the other person is focused on what is being said and they give credit to those who watch their mouth and pick up on their body language. If you need a Healer to pay instant attention to a comment, start by stating how you feel about the task.

TIPS FOR HEALERS, FOR WHEN THEY DEAL WITH OTHERS.

Healer vs Healer

Healers love to be around each other. They all understand that the world can be a lovely place to be. Through their joint effort, they can make it better, providing people open up and put some emotion on show. Healers do attract other like-minded souls as if they can sense each other's openness and they drift in the same direction, meeting up at chance opportunities. Healers get on great with one another, but they tend to separate to join other groups, so that they can share the love. When they do come together, it will feel like a very supporting and safe environment to be in. They will chat about how they helped others; some may call it gossip, but it is more of a support for each other as a Healer will often look to offload their concerns to another Healer. They are comfortable knowing that a caring response will be given and they will feel secure to tell others of their more intimate secrets.

When a Healer goes into competition with another Healer, they will support each other throughout and even hold hands as they cross the finishing line. Neither Healer will show that they want to win. Instead they are coy about the situation and instead of celebrating, they will comfort the looser. When Healers get together, they will find something to chat about for hours. They will continue until they are completely exhausted or they have run out of time.

Healers will always support each other and want to be best friends, even if they do not have the same interests. They will not be pushing their own agendas, but instead they will be asking for more details. If a Healer falls out with another Healer, they will not be apart for long, unless it is was a massive emotional upset. They will quickly forgive and forget.

Healer vs Hunter

Healers and Hunters are both very open and they enjoy the freedom of using feelings and emotions in any conversation. They can be good friends and will work well together. They will both use their gut instinct and will get good results, especially if they both value a task and it being worthwhile.

The Hunter is the more dominant person and will put pressure on the Healer.

This tends to happen when the majority of the work has been complete and the Hunter loses interest in finishing off the small details. Healers are happy to finish off a task, providing the Hunter gives them some credit for doing it. A Hunter can recognise a Healer's skills, even when they are glory hunting, but only if they connect with the Healer during the task. The Hunter can be dismissive to a Healer telling them not to bother with small details, but during those last few finishing touches, a Healer will change the dynamics of a team slowly, placing the burden onto the Healer so they can move on. Healers want Hunters to make the same level of commitment to any task but they are intuitive enough to recognise their dedication to detail is better than the Hunters, so they may not say anything that will cause an argument.

If a Healer wants to improve relationships and communication with a Hunter, they have to set clear boundaries from the start and keep reminding the Hunter when they try to change it. Hunters are loyal but being they are an Air element, it is difficult to pin them down and a Healer may just give up. A Hunter will not do 'subtle' and no hint no matter how big will be picked up by them. It is out of a Healer's comfort zone to set boundaries, but without them, the relationship will suffer.

Hunters will appreciate Healers being able to stand up for themselves and will do what they are told, providing the boundaries are not extended.

Healer vs Protector

Healers and Protectors are the complete opposites of each other. The dominant Protector against the caring Healer actually brings a wonderful blend of friendship. If a Healer is being taken advantage of, a Protector has no problem recognising this, and will step in to look after them. A Healer will give emotional guidance to a Protector on subtle matters. A Healer can take the sharp edges off any Protector, making them more approachable and appear friendly. If friends, a Healer will ignore a Protector's bluntness, knowing it is not the Protector's intention to be that way. The Protector's stubbornness is also managed well by a Healer, as they can make a Protector see reason through sharing their emotions. Healers see Protectors as the efficient, no messing individual, but they can push the situation when they constantly try to get them to open up.

A Healer and a Protector can have differences in opinion. The Protector, not being interested in emotion and gut feelings, can dismiss the Healer's need to feel these things as they make their plans. A Healer can feel that a relationship can be all 'one-way' and if this happens, they will only put up with so much before they push their button.

For a Healer to improve a relationship with a Protector, they need to stop worrying about emotions in a Protector and accept what they are shown as a Protector will show emotion, but in a completely different way. If they spend time with a Protector, they will recognise subtle differences when a Protector deals with others. Although a Protector does not appear to be concerned about how a Healer is feeling, they do need to know that a Healer is part of the team. If a Healer wants more input from a Protector, they need to ask for it, but they have to get to the point fast.

Healer vs Gatherer

Healers and Gatherers are both indirect tribe members. They both like detail and chatting about the small stuff, which others will think as unimportant. The relationship between a Healer and Gatherer can be quite good, providing that the Gatherer does not ask too many "How..." or "What if..." questions of the Healer. The friction happens when the openness of a Healer's emotions interferes with the closed nature of the Gatherer.

Healers use their emotions and gut instincts too much for a Gatherer's liking; they want fact. The Gatherer wants a carefully thought-out plan and detail of how the Healer is going to get that result. A Healer will not be able to provide as much detail as the Gatherer wants, and they can be considered to be away with the fairies. If a Healer needs to get into the good books of a Gatherer, they need to write stuff down and show it as a process. A Gatherer will pull the result apart, wanting to see the individual functions, not out of spite, but to work out how it was done. This will cause upset to a Healer and they can feel belittled. These small misunderstandings can cause real upset; the Healer will feel unappreciated and the Gatherer does not understand why they are upset.

If a Healer wants to improve their relationship with a Gatherer, they need to be aware of their logical minds. If they start to give running updates of progress to a Gatherer, it will stop the Gatherer from interfering and pulling apart the final result. If a Healer needs to write a report or attend a meeting run by a Gatherer, they need to leave emotion out of it. Sticking to the facts and projected results, showing processes of how they are to be obtained, will please a Gatherer. The Gatherer will see that the Healer is being more thoughtful and process driven and give extra leeway in their work.

11. A TRIBE THAT WORKS.

Get the most from any tribe.

People want to be part of a hard-working and successful tribe. Tribes are full of different types of people. Most of us know that some tribes work better than others, and some don't work at all. There have been occasions when tribes have had such bad infighting, they acquire a bad reputation. These bad tribes are allowed to grow, infecting other tribes, and eventually they affect an entire organisation, family or social group.

Using the CTS and then recognising the character traits within a tribe, as in who are the Hunters, Protectors, Gatherers and Healers, will help improve interactions and communication between them. Sharing the information in this book with others will help them understand issues around personality clashes and will help them become a more understanding tribe member. It does get easier with practice, and providing people are willing to give it a go, instant results can be seen. Before we delve into team building exercises, strapping oil drums together and trying to cross a muddy lake, I want to make a quick point about dealing with individuals in a tribe. It is all about communication. The point I want to make has already been made by Professor Mehrabian. He combined two studies along with their results, and came up with a rule about communication. It is not all about the spoken or written word, as this is only 7% of the interaction. There is the voice to consider; its pitch, too loud, too soft, too high or too low, which accounts for 38%. Then you have the body language, which he stated accounted for the last 55%.

My point is simple. When sending an email to someone, you are only using 7% of the available communication ability to make the point. If an impact is required when making a statement, human interaction provides the other 93%, so if it is an important matter, do it face-to-face.

Enough about numbers; we can put our calculators away again. Before we get on to building the perfect tribe, I already know what you are thinking. That you want to fill your own tribe with the same character trait as yourself, is that right?

Let us have a look at this theory before you make your mind up. I was once part of a team that was sent to carry out an operation using specialist training that I had been given. It was a few days away from home and the attachment was an exciting prospect. I turned up at work with my overnight bags packed and collected my work equipment that I was going to need. I went to the vehicle yard and I found the rest of my team preparing the vehicle. At the time, although

I knew every one of these people that were coming away with me, I had no idea what made them tick and more to the point, I was not interested. We had a three-hour drive and all of us had a great time; there was lots of laughing and shouting going on, but we were all prepared to do the 'job' when we arrived.

Things were going great. After the first shift had finished and we had completed the tasks we had been set, we went to the hotel in which we were to be sleeping in. All of us wanted to tell our 'victory' story on the journey there. Things got a little loud and people were butting in and trying to get the praise for doing 'this' or doing 'that'. It quite annoying and people were getting angry. Looking back on this operation, and knowing what I now know, I now realise that I had gone away with a team full of Hunters. After three days, none of us were enjoying the company any more. We finally got back to our station and we could barely say goodbye to each other without feeling some resentment for not being the focus of the group.

Had I not had this experience, I may not of been able to put my CTS to good practice. Going away with like-minded, similar thought processing individuals sounds like fun. It should mean there was no end of throwing caution to the wind and getting on with the task at hand, with little instruction.

However, once the glory of the task had been completed, there was no one to clear up after us.

No one wanted to write the report, unless it was about them, no one wanted to make a plan for the next day, what time to meet for breakfast and what time to leave; it was all played by 'ear'. We were never late and we accomplished what we had been asked to do, but there was a lot of stress involved. It also get a little repetitive hearing, "I'm the best," all the time, even when it came to discussing how many sausages someone was able to cram into their sandwich. The same applies for tribe full of Protectors. They will take on as many tasks as they can, as they are the only ones who can do it properly. Without someone looking after them, they will all get 'burn-out'. They will snipe at each other for not doing as much as the other, and they will all push their buttons getting more and more wound up. A group of Protectors need to be fed and not be allowed to gorge. Recognising each of their achievements is a must, otherwise they lose interest and will go elsewhere.

A group of Gatherers have another problem. They need to know as much detail as possible before they start anything, and if you want them to do anything fast, forget it. They will bicker and fight for the top spot and this can turn nasty, with individual Gatherers going off to do just 'their' bit.

After they have completed their work, they will inspect the other tribe members' contributions, and all this takes time.

Healers just want to feel that they are part of a tribe. They will make sure that the other Healers are all well looked after in the group. None of them will be particularly interested in taking charge, and there will be a certain amount of guess work and 'gut feelings' going on. They will be the happiest team, but little quantifiable work will be achieved.

Modern-day Cavemen no longer stay within their own groups. Work has changed; it is now more complicated than ever. There is more paperwork, more responsibility than there ever used to be. There is no longer a principle task; jobs expect people to fulfil a whole range of different tasks that need multiple skills and abilities. People no longer have one soul responsibility to go off hunting, watching the tribe, gathering plenty of stocks and supplies or healing the sick. Today's farmers need to be business focused, the police no longer only deal with rule breaking, doctors need to write long reports. All of these and many more roles are now no longer about the 'job' or the work involved; it is about being accountable and being able to justify any or no action to be taken.

Regardless of what the task or job, there is no longer a 'fixed' personality trait to complete that given role. So many jobs and roles have all the elements that the four tribe members possess. From the job that we hold down to pay the bills to the family and parenting requirements that we undertake, mixing and matching traits makes the best possible use of the combination tribe members can bring.

The need to keep all the same members together no longer fits modern-day living. The way that a modern business operates means that they must employ a mixed tribe. The right combination of people will provide all of the elements needed for it to be successful. The mixtures of personalities will give the broadest, best blend of character traits.

The personal and home lives of many people now no longer allows for the female to stay at home and undertake the sole responsibility of bringing up the children and to take care of the home. This is now a shared responsibility and the personality traits have to be broad enough to cover all of the needs in the home. Where there are any shortfalls, problems will arise from these areas.

The skill of managing a mixed team of different traits is hard. Like a blended whiskey, too much of one malt can ruin a perfectly good drink. A team needs a good balance of all the characters in the tribe. It is not necessary to have a 25% balance across the team; some team roles will need more of one trait than another.

Not many people can build an effective team from scratch; most people either form a group through necessity or inherit a tribe that has already been put together.

If someone has concerns about a tribe or someone recognises that their own tribe is not performing correctly, or there are clashes happening within it on a regular basis, then we need to assess the tribe.

List all the names in the tribe on a piece of paper and carefully work out their character trait, giving them their own personal label from the CTS. If there are too many of one tribal trait, then this may be the cause of some friction or it lacking direction. Depending on the type of problem that needs addressing, this chart could help guide you to assess the problem.

We all know that there has never been a one size that fits all but people have believed that equal rights has meant that we have to treat everyone the same. What we should be doing is treating everyone differently, on how they need to be treated.

Concern	Possible Resolve
Too many tasks outstanding	More Protectors are needed
Paperwork always late or incorrect	More Gatherers will be required
Jobs not getting done quickly enough	Use more Hunters
People feeling unsupported or undervalued	Put more Healers into the mix
Things not up to standard	More Protectors and Gatherers required
Low Morale	Add some Healers and Hunters
Lack of direction	Put more Hunters and Protectors into the tribe
Lack of planning	More Healers and Gatherers needed

People who are part of a tribe need to be aware of each other's different personality traits. Do not treat them all the same. We all need to be constantly changing our communication style, giving different amounts of information to each other, all based on the other person's personality trait.

I have been in many new car showrooms and seen this 'one size fits all' mentality many times. Some sales assistants have tried to speak to me as if I have never driven a car before and others hide away until I ask for help, then they go straight into the numbers game, with no interest of showing me the car.

Using the CTS and identifying the correct Caveman character profile will help people recognise each individual member of a tribe. Communicating and dealing with them as tribal individuals, based on their CTS label, will produce some very different and extraordinary results.

If a tribe is not functioning, be aware of the people who may want to watch a real-life Buckaroo game, not being interested in getting the tribe to work in harmony. In which case, move away from them.

If we follow simple rules, such as never asking a Gatherer and a Hunter to work together, or trying to micromanage a Protector or getting a Healer to work alone, it will be of benefit to the entire tribe.

If you want to know where to start, treat a tribe member with their most dominant trait, and it will get a different result. Never be afraid to change a label if we get it wrong (think about the 'Nature vs Nurture' element). Experiment with all the labels as the effort invested in working out your work colleagues, friends and family members will be paid back in no time at all.

We all want less stress in our lives. Give our bodies less opportunity to push our buttons by living in a harmonious tribe. Crack each other's code and find that we all become more tolerant of 'their' obvious failings.

Take time to assess the last time you spoke to someone; label them and the next time you meet, you will already be thinking of their thought process and be able to start guessing what their reactions will be.

Be more interactive. Shaking hands with people when you meet them allows a more intimate and immediate assessment of their character trait. Point to note; you cannot shake hands with someone from a keyboard.

People who email the entire office with important information believing they are being 'efficient' and 'quick' are missing the point about how humans operate and the need for interaction.

One last story before I move on to the final important point about getting a tribe to work in harmony. In my workplace, e-learning or 'NCALT' has been introduced. When a new important piece of legislation comes into force, it needs to be quickly assimilated into the daily operational practices of my work and that of my colleagues. The use of e-learning was the vessel that was to deliver these vitally important updates to the 1,000 members of the organisation who work there.

A new NCALT package is released every month or so, and takes around an hour to complete. Remember, only 7% of an affective message is delivered by words alone and an hour staring at a screen is not healthy and is not an exciting prospect. How does an organisation present these important training sessions, weighing up costs, time and the ability to deliver training to so many people, without the need to abstract them from their workplace? It is a difficult question, and one I cannot answer.

Would you trust a doctor that has completed his entire training sat in front of a computer? How would a football or basketball player fair in a game if they did all their training in front of a screen? If I were to be asked what I have learnt from any of these packages, or even recall what the title was of the last one I have completed or even what it was all about, I would disappoint the person asking. My focus is to finish the package and put a tick in the box, not to learn anything. However, the last face-to-face training that I attended was carried out in Bristol. I can remember who I was with, what the trainers spoke about, and I can recall the entire day's activities and input. I took a lot of information away with me that day, and none of it was written down.

Like many offices or places of work, an information giving email that is sent out is either deleted, or worse, put straight into a junk folder. The sender does not count how many people have read the message; their job is done. They will assume everyone has digested the content.

Important information that is vital to the operational effectiveness to a tribe should never be passed by electronic means. The only tribe member that gains any benefit from these inputs (albeit very little) are the Gatherers, the hoarders of the tribe. They will have filed the message away in a 'useful' folder somewhere, never to be looked at again.

To sum up, we need to communicate better. We need to treat everyone differently referring to their own CTS label. Take time to speak to people and watch what the results are.

After using these simple and now obvious techniques, start labelling the first few tribe members. Be more personable with others and stop sending so many emails; things will get easier with practice and there will be a reduction in number of times stress buttons are pushed at home, at work and in our social occasions.

PART THREE

217

12. CHANGE

No one likes Change.

Our Caveman ancestors never had to deal with Change. They were too busy Hunting Mammoths, Gathering firewood, Protecting the tribe or Healing the sick and injured. The only Change they knew was the change of weather.

They did not know what the word 'future' meant and never had to worry about any changes. They lived for each and every day, and knew what their purpose in life was. They only got stressed when they had to use their fight or flight reflex. Starting from primitive beginnings, the Caveman grew in skills and knowledge and became the dominant creature of this planet. I bet they never knew that was going to happen.

Our ancestors would not cope with the level of change we now face every day. We have so many changes going on in our lives, we only want to add to them by making more 'life' choices; what to wear, which new mobile to get, what will we have for lunch... the list is endless.

Our Caveman ancestors never had to worry about diets, or experience the stress of running out of battery on a mobile phone, or having to make other arrangements when they got stuck at work, being made redundant from their job or changes being made to their role in the tribe.

Change can be a positive thing as long as it is kept into perspective; moving from 'normal' to 'medicated' shampoo is not stressful, but it is Change. Moving house can be an exciting time, but it has also been dubbed as one of the most stressful times we can experience in our lives. Change brings on stress, especially when the change has been forced upon us.

When we do not expect Change or we are forced to accept it, it becomes a massive button pusher. These stressful situations at work, at home or in our social lives can push people over the edge.

If we put some of today's choices and changes into the lives of our Caveman ancestors, how would they cope doing the same job? Would Health and Safety training get in their way of feeding or protecting the tribe? How many ways do they need to know of how to hunt a Mammoth?

What would happen if the Caveman could suddenly order a Mammoth online and get it delivered in a time slot of their choosing? Which spear could they order? Which one has the best reviews and best deals? These modern-day changes were designed to make our lives easier, but have in fact made them more complicated as now we have to choose which one is best. The stress added to making a choice, making sure we get the best deal, is it the right one to get, or is there something better out there?

Choice and Change is a modern-day stress factor and it is regularly overlooked and ignored by many of us. We manage stress on a daily basis, pushing our buttons when plans suddenly change. There are so many elements that need to be addressed that this book could go on forever, so it has been created to deal with the big one, 'forced' Change or 'need' for Change.

Delivering the message of Change can have a massive impact on how people perceive the concern. Just as above, when using the word 'need' instead of 'force', it makes all the difference when delivering the message. Communication is one key element to managing Change successfully. How to manage our own expectations, how to see Change as a positive step and how we handle it, is what this part of the book is all about.

We all need to reduce the number of times we push our stress buttons. Change is the hardest area for us to manage, especially when it is needed. The reason most people do not like Change, is because with Change comes uncertainty. Stressful Change can reoccur within us and can last for ages. Once we think we have mastered the change, something will happen and it will trigger it off again.

When a change is needed, it can be a disruptive process; it will take people's attention away from where it is needed and place it on the change process instead.

We all want 'quick' fixes in our lives, but what is really needed are a few 'mindset' adjustments to keep things in perspective. Things to consider;

- Do we live to work or work to live? We spend eight to ten hours a day at work, five days a week. A massive part of our adult life spent doing what someone else tells us to do. It is 'just a job.'

  No matter what we do for work, it is only a job and jobs can and do Change. We work only so we can get paid for us to have a life. Does anyone want to drag work worries home with them, grumbling and worrying, rather than spending it with the family?

- Without good employees, there will be no business.

This is just to make you realise how important you are in your workplace. Although you may think that work has all the control, without your professionalism, experience, qualifications and drive to do the best you can, your company would not be as successful as it is.

- Are we focusing on the challenge of Change, or on the end result?

No matter what the change is from losing a few pounds, getting fitter or finding a new job, we put our focus on the future rather than the here and now. Knowing that we can only change a moment at a time helps us achieve the desired end result.

- What control do we have of Change?

Some Changes cannot be controlled. There can be no point in fighting Change, especially when acceptance can be more beneficial. However, when lifestyle choices are important and we have to change, then we can own it and reduce resistance and stress in the same process.

Change needs to be appealing; we have to find the right angle to view it from. It needs to make us want to Change, not fear it and put up resistance. The way to make Change more appetising is to appeal to our emotional thoughts, instead of our rational brains.

We become quite selfish when there is a need for change and do not ask the right questions; we all concentrate on the negative and on how it will affect 'me'. We should be concentrating on the positives of Change, finding out the more appealing parts of why it is required, and supporting it; it is far less stressful. Without all the correct information, how are we to make a proper decision about what is best for us?

When we are in groups, we become herd animals. If there are more negative people than positive in a herd, we will follow their lead, jumping on the negative bandwagon. We feel safe to agree with a crowd and let our emotional Mammoth off the lead, worrying later when we have to catch it again.

Change has a dirty underbelly as people love rumours and gossip. They can thrive on making someone the bad person. Cast your mind back when someone you know has tried to do some exercise or make a positive change in their lives; have you fully supported them, or have you made fun from behind their back?

Accepting Change, and understanding that others will get scared when you want to change, can reduce the stress and stop the button from being pressed. Taking control of our Mammoth, and making Change a personal effort to find out what it really means, is the first real step everyone should take. Tell others why Change is important, but never share the details of a goal. By all means, tell people you want to lose weight, but never tell them you want to lose three stone.

Part of using the Caveman Change Principles is about having time for personal reflection. I am not saying strip down to your undies, cross your legs and then repeat a mantra. It is about having some personal time and not being afraid of taking some time for 'you' during this time. If you need to, 'accidentally' leave your mobile at home when you go to the gym or a class. It will feel funny at first, but trust me; you will not die because of it.

Although I am not a doctor, I am happy to say that your life does not depend on having a mobile phone in your pocket or by your side 24 hours a day, unless by the time you read this book, they have already invented some form of pacemaker app, in which case put the phone on to airplane mode.

To show you how Caveman Change can work, a really simple change can be being without your mobile phone or switching it off for a period of time. Not just putting it on silent, but seeing the screen ask "Are you sure?" before it goes blank for at least 30 minutes a day will give people back a sense of real freedom. This may be the Change you want to introduce or, "Stop taking my mobile to bed," or, "I will show my partner as much attention as I do my mobile." That last one is not going to help the relationship if you want to keep them plugged in all the time.

Think about it; nothing can be done when you are asleep, and the reality of knowing that something that is 'alive' is on the bedside table does not allow for a restful sleep. This is the 'understanding' of the need for Change.

Doing the Change allows you to have personal space to develop and helps to relax the mind, making you less stressed, better rested and not dependent on a piece of technology. This is the Future of the Change.

Change can be stressful or fun. It is only in the eye of the person who sees it as an advancement or an incumbent function that chooses the emotion attached to the Change. New Year's resolutions are promised by millions every 1st January and then failed by 14th January, as people no longer believe in them. We want to improve our lives, our health or our wealth, and then nothing happens. We fail right at the beginning, and this failure ends up pushing our buttons, as we have another eleven months and two weeks left on our year-long gym membership. We see the promised resolution slip away and believe it is just another personal failure, all because we have failed to understand Change.

Without Change, we would all still be living in caves, and Apple would be something that only grew on trees. We would never have invented televisions; our Friday night shows would be us sat in front of a badly-drawn picture of a Mammoth on one of the walls of our cave.

Changes have to have a fundamental element that it has to have a benefit, and be exciting and fun for it to succeed.

The failure to Change is the biggest button presser causing all stress and not the Change itself. When we see no improvement to our personal circumstances, we feel cheated and our stress levels rise when we start to believe that Change is pointless. We have to stop seeing the word 'Change' as a dirty, evil word. It should have a welcoming feel to it.

Switching the focus of Change from a process function to an emotional one, will help Change happen. We fail to change when we have no emotional attachment, and our hearts were never truly involved.

Taking control of the things that matter to us and recognising they are within our power to change will reduce stress. This part of the book will walk anyone through the Caveman Change Principles, helping them understand Change and unlock a few ideas of how to improve our lives through Change.

～

13. THE CAVEMAN HERDER AND THE PET MAMMOTH

The right and left parts of our brain.

The Caveman Change Principles is about keeping it simple; it does not use medical jargon or complex psychology studies. It is a simple way to help explain how the soft, squishy stuff in most of our heads work when it comes to change management. The principle is simple, as it refers to a Caveman Herder and the pet Mammoth, who both reside upstairs in our thinking machine. It explains how we see, understand and then ultimately how to be able to deal with Change.

Imagine what that could mean, to have control over a desired or much-needed Change in our day-to-day life. It would mean a reduction in the number of button presses we have to endure each day, and less stress to boot.

Starting at the beginning, we have to first accept a new theory. You will have heard the saying, "Are you following your head or your heart?" Well the Caveman Change Principle uses a similar idea, except there is a Caveman Herder and a pet Mammoth. There is only 'head' and no 'heart', so perhaps it is not similar at all, but bear with me.

229

The head and the heart have been given to mean the thought process and the separate emotions attached respectively. Even though we all know that emotions happen in the brain and not in the heart, it is a saying that fits a meaning.

Psychologists believe that there are two sides to our brain, rather than one big muscle that fits in the cavity of our noggin. It is split down the middle into a left and a right side. Just to mention about being right or left handed, this book has been written for the majority of right-handed readers, so if you feel the need, please take a pencil and cross through right and left, and replace it with left and right.

The typical left side of our brain has long believed to be our logical, analytical side, where all the planning is done, the 'Thinker' side of the brain. This is the side where our Caveman Herder lives.

Our Herder likes to try and make sense of the world around us; with fast and analytical thinking ability, the Herder can get us out of bother. The Herder will look at all the information available and make a split-second, reasoned, rationalised opinion based on the new information.

The Herder has an amazing talent of jumping to conclusions and barrelling into situations, jumping in with both feet and changing direction all the time. Regardless of which character you are in the CTS, this Herder is everyone's Hunter, a conscience, sat on our shoulder telling us what to do, wanting us to act on its impulse reaction. The Herder side looks after all the tricky stuff in our head, like language functions, reading, writing, and the ability to speak along with interpreting any literal meanings during a complex conversation.

The typical right side of our brain is where we do our intuitive and emotional bits, also known as the 'Doer' side. This is where the Herder's pet Mammoth lives.

The Mammoth likes to look after all the emotional stuff, from loving something, to hating and fearing it as well.

The Mammoth is much slower to appreciate fast-paced decisions and so does not like fast change.

The Mammoth enjoys repetition and getting cheap thrills. This is why the Mammoth can become addicted to the wrong things, such as caffeine, sugar, gambling or being sat on the sofa. The Mammoth is a lazy creature, and when it gets caught in a bad cycle of behaviour, it is very difficult to get it to do anything else. The brain Mammoth is very skittish, scared of its own shadow, and needs to be treated with a lot of care.

Caveman Change Principles can also be used to tackle individual fears. Where people have phobias, these are kept in the Mammoth side of the brain. The Mammoth, being a complete coward, does not tackle these issues, but instead allows them to fester in the corner of our minds, not brave enough to tackle the source of this panic.

A phobia manifests when someone has either been taught or experienced a terrifying ordeal. From my own experience, I can remember as a child climbing a ladder that was left at the side of our old house whilst the window cleaner got some bits from his van. I could get to the very top of the ladder and back down without an ounce of fear.

Then I remember being caught by my mother when I was at the top. She screamed and shouted at me when I was stood right at the very top. The knowing of being caught, the panic I felt because I became scared when I was shouted at, did something to me. When I got back to ground level, she scolded me for doing something that was incredibly dangerous. That fear I felt being at the top was not from ladders, but it linked itself to the circumstances. Later I was scolded again by my father, who unknown to me had a fear of ladders.

In my head, the Mammoth has linked both the scaldings to the ladder incident and it suddenly had an irrational fear of ladders. This fear that I felt, being caught doing something I should not have been doing, meant I have not been able to get six feet off the ground on any ladder before my knees start to knock. This fear can be conquered, and using the Caveman Change Principles, I have made progress. Although my Mammoth still gets scared from time to time, ladders are no longer a massive phobia.

The Caveman Herder and the Mammoth are completely opposite characters. They both have to come to an agreement to make any Change become a lasting habit. Here is a simple, short exercise to get an understanding of this fear, and to experience a forced Change.

Imagine you need a pint of milk; it is a regular occurrence and you stroll to the shops. You leave the house and walk the same route to the shop. At the shop, you know where the milk is, how much it is, and recognise where the till area is, and probably who is serving. Then once the transaction is complete, you return home, using the same footpaths and crossing the same roads. It is a well-known journey, and it can be done without even thinking about it. This is where the Mammoth is most comfortable.

Now the same scenario; you need a pint of milk but our regular shop is closed for the day so we have to use another shop. The Herder takes over and decides that we have to work out a new route, one that probably goes in the opposite direction to a new shop. With new roads and new neighbourhoods to walk through, it is a different feeling to the old comfortably-timed walk as before. This feeling of Change is uncomfortable. The Mammoth does not like it. When the new shop has been located, we have now hunt for the milk aisle and then find out if the price is different.

Next is finding the till and wondering if the cashier is as happy as the one in the other shop. Once the milk has been paid for, we have to now negotiate the strange journey back home, constantly wondering if this is the best route to use. The Mammoth is so far out its comfort zone, it has gone into panic mode; it does not like.

When we get home, because the Mammoth has been pushing the button all the way there and back, we are exhausted and vow never to go back to that new shop ever again, only wishing that our old regular shop is open again tomorrow.

The above exercise is the easiest way to understand how Change can fail to happen. Only when both the Caveman and the pet Mammoth agree to a change will a commitment be made and Change has a chance of happening. If they both want a change to stick, rather than just a one-off visit to a new shop, then they have to do it together, or it will not happen. This reasoning is why so many New Year resolutions fail, because only the Caveman agrees to the change, leaving the Mammoth out of the plan so the Mammoth gets scared, meaning it will fail.

As the exercise shows, change is a new map, a new journey, and a new destination. We have to get both the Herder and the Mammoth on a new path to the new destination.

If we are comfortable sat on the sofa and then suddenly want to look like a beach model, one visit to the gym is not going to be enough. We have to plan, research and agree to a course of action, rather than jumping in with both feet.

The Herder is able to think things through and see the logical reason for any change. They plan for the immediate need, but not really for the long term. They are very excitable and have difficulty in containing this new buzz they feel. They become quite loud and become the voice of reason in our heads. Their impatient nature, wanting to try new things all the time, means that their long-term outlook is only a dream, and with dreams we can have new ones every night.

The pet Mammoth is a lot slower and sceptical of change so needs time to prepare and come to terms with this new idea of change. The Mammoth thrives on learnt behaviour. They like to do the same things over and over. They get caught in a comfortable rut, walking the same path day after day, doing the same thing week after week.

If a Mammoth has gotten used to walking a path, probably to the sofa after work, sitting and watching television, then this has become its normal habit and behaviour. This is the comfortable rut.

The failure of change happens when we listen to our Herder and force ourselves to pack a gym bag. We force the Mammoth off the comfortable sofa, and force ourselves to the sweaty, noisy building where we beast ourselves until we can no longer stand up.

The Mammoth has not understood why we are doing this and really does not see this as being any fun. It just wants to get back into that comfortable rut.

Our Herder needs the Mammoth to understand why this change is needed, but they cannot use the same excitement and logical thinking that they used to come to their own conclusion, because the Mammoth is not interested. Unless the Mammoth 'feels' a benefit, it will not be interested; it has to have an emotional understanding, not a logical one. Hitting our Mammoth's emotions is easy, but there is a process to learn first. We can forget using the logical side, as the Herder has already used it, to convince us Change is needed. We have to concentrate on motivating the Mammoth.

The Herder can help by calming down and not racing ahead, as both the Herder and the Mammoth need to walk the new path together. If the Herder looses the Mammoth, it will get stressed and run off, returning to the comfortable rut.

We need time to convince the Mammoth that Change is good, that when Change does happen, it has a real benefit to us. The use of emotion to suggest a change will hit the Mammoth right in its gut, so that it has to take notice.

It needs to be a strong emotion to hit it in the sweet spot, with it feeling the full impact of why Change is necessary. A good example of hitting the emotional spot is the use of family intervention, when children plea with their parents for Change, using every emotion they can, tugging at the heart strings forcing the parents' Mammoth to accept Change.

When it comes to protecting others, our Mammoths do not need to be convinced, they can make instant changes, especially when it comes to children. This emotional weakness can be exploited if we want to use it forcing the Mammoth to accept Change.

The problem is that having children is an expensive option and you are stuck with them for 18 years, when all you want to do is lose a little bit of weight. Our Herder needs to become that child, stop overthinking things, and stop trying to use logic on the Mammoth. If the Herder does not start playing the game, they will easily lose the Mammoth.

The Mammoth is a three-ton beast and it takes a lot of effort for it to do anything, so the effort needs to be worthwhile. Remember, the Mammoth is lazy and skittish. The Mammoth wants quick wins, so to convince it to do something is going to take time and effort.

When we do not get the Mammoth to engage (emotionally), problems can happen when the Herder goes off at the logical end. They are full of motivation; they start off being full of energy, wanting to stride off down the new path, the path that is going to take them to a new destination, where it means a 'happier you'. The Herder is our 'willpower'; they are not interested in wasting time talking about it and do not speak to the Mammoth. Instead, the Herder grabs hold of the Mammoth and pushes it out the door. The Herder starts to shove the Mammoth down the new path. The Herder uses every bit of strength they have to get the Mammoth on the path.

Once the Mammoth is on the right path, the Herder continues to shove and push the Mammoth up the path; they are our 'willpower' fighting the change head on.

Just like willpower, the Herder will run out of energy, ending up exhausted. Now the Mammoth is not being pushed or shoved around, it feels nervous; it has to start thinking for itself and it has no idea what to do. The reason for the change has not been explained to the Mammoth and it feels lost, starting to panic. The Mammoth does exactly what is expected of it — it goes back to what feels normal, in comfortable surroundings; it runs all the way back down the new path it has just been shoved up, and back into its familiar rut.

Every time Change fails, it will be because our Mammoth gave up, either because it was forced, only half-heartedly, to engage with it, or the Herder gets impatient and goes on ahead, leaving the Mammoth alone and scared.

We need to convince both the Mammoth and the Herder that they are in it together and have to work in partnership.

Change has to have a common goal. Both the Herder and the Mammoth have to understand it before they set off down the path in a new direction. The Mammoth has to be convinced it is worthy of it, stepping out of its comfort zone and into the potential danger and possible failure.

The Mammoth cannot be blamed when it was never shown or involved in the planning of the route to changing the final destination. If it did not know why the change was needed, then how is it going to know where to go to improve its life? The Mammoth will never be as concerned about Change as the Herder will be. It will try and slip past the Herder for that 'one last cigarette' or the old 'I'll start tomorrow' trick. The Mammoth needs to be reminded why it is on the new path and not allowed to return to the old comfortable path by allowing it to light up another cigarette or getting back on the sofa when it should be going to the gym.

Watch out for the false trails marked 'shortcut'; these are Change traps. They are set like honeytraps, wanting to catch the Herder. There has to be consistency in the plan so the Mammoth does not get spooked, stick to the route.

These shortcuts are dotted all the way along a new route, and they try to entice Herders into changing their direction going off the route they had agreed with the Mammoth.

These Change traps get our Herder very excited, making them want to change the agreed plans immediately. They can see all the benefits of the new Change, doing more, trying a new routine, all in a bid to shorten the agreed journey and get to the destination faster, and they forget about the Mammoth.

The Herder will change the direction of the path again in another new direction, and not tell the Mammoth. It might be a simple change of day going to the gym, or a new stop smoking aid that has a shinier label or funnier shape than the last one. Whatever it might be, the Mammoth will not like it if it is not involved in the discussion to change the route.

The smallest of Changes after the Mammoth has committed itself to a new path has the potential of spooking the Mammoth and it will run back to the old path, making the Change fail.

Our Herder can lose the new path when they get distracted, but can return to it again quickly, providing they are reminded they have stepped off the planned route. If this does happen, the Herder has to check on the Mammoth's welfare, reassure it and hope that they have not already lost it.

The Mammoth is a huge creature so there is little wonder why a tiny Herder can only control it for so long. If the Mammoth manages to return to its old comfortable path, the Herder will have to follow it back, becoming disheartened and probably giving up as well. The Herder will be upset, angry, stressed and overwhelmed from any failure, and will need time to calm down.

Our Herder does not need to use all their energy to push the Mammoth around; instead, they need to learn how to lead it. The next chapter explains how this is done.

Providing we can get the Herder to slow down, understand how the Mammoth thinks using its emotions, and then how to use those emotions, the Herder can motivate it and lead the Mammoth down the new path.

Any Change can be a long slog. Putting effort into detailing the new path, including the Mammoth's feelings from the beginning, means Change has a greater possibility of success.

Get a clean notepad out and start to write down a set of instructions. The Herder will help with the logical why, but concentrate on how it will make you feel when you get the destination, the emotional why. Clearly define a route, think of it as a map, and jot your expected journey out on the pad. The next few chapters will help you do this. In doing these things, it is showing the Mammoth what to expect. It will help to unite the Herder and the Mammoth, and steer them both to the new destination.

Stick to the plan; do not scare the Mammoth and the route must not change. Do not get tempted with a Change trap; the only shortcut you will find is the one that leads back to the beginning.

14. PLAN THE ROUTE

Have a clearly defined route.

Change is hard so you have to be totally committed. Going through a Change needs to be treated as if we are going on an unknown journey to a new and exotic location. What do we need to pack? Do we need any jabs? What currency do they use? What language do they speak? And the most important question, how are we going to get there?

The journey is taken by both the Herder and the Mammoth in unison. The Herder has worked out why the Change is needed, and now we have to convince the Mammoth that the journey is worthwhile. We do this in two stages; first, we show the Mammoth what is involved in the Change by mapping it, and second we draw a picture of the destination, which is covered in the next chapter.

To convince the Mammoth that Change is needed, we have to show it that there is a plan, that if we follow the plan we can reach the new destination and the Change will have taken place. When it recognises that the plan can work, we hit it with the emotion reasons with the picture in the following chapter, and get it to start moving straight away.

We have to include and think about the Mammoth's reactions throughout the planning process. We have to convince the Herder that they must do it with the Mammoth, otherwise it will fail.

From the very first inkling of an idea for Change, we need to start to plan it. Writing it down clearly in a chronological order in front of us, allows the Mammoth to watch and, hopefully, capture its interest. The plan needs to be written out and put somewhere where it can be checked, updated and, once agreed, stuck to.

By doing this, we are showing the Mammoth that there is a plan and we have got a desired route that we want to follow to the new destination. We need to get the Mammoth to become desensitised with the idea of Change and not to scare it by dropping the whole idea on it out of the blue.

The very first thing we need to do is to do some self-reflection, like my ladder story. Think back to when the Mammoth first got scared and wanted to stay in its comfortable rut. Was the eating habit caused by bullies or having kids? Was the smoking caused by watching parents smoke or the caffeine addiction caused by copying people at work? There should be at least one trigger that started the Mammoth on its comfortable path.

246

If you can identify that trigger, it will help the Change process and will form part of the planning stage.

The plan should include the exact Change wanted, such as:

- to give up smoking forever
- to be able to run five miles non-stop
- to lose two stone
- to stop gambling
- to grow my fingernails
- to be able to climb a ladder without fear

The plan needs to be declared in a positive statement and not in the negative. A plan should not start with a "I will not…" The Mammoth is lazy and not always attentive to what is being said, written or read. It may miss the first part and only hear the last bit which is, "…eat any more chocolate."

Writing "I will not chew my fingernails" is dangerous, whereas stating it positively like, "I will grow my fingernails," is much better, as even a lazy Mammoth can ignore the first two words and still get the same meaning.

The Reason Change is needed:

- so I can breathe better and become healthier
- so I can smell fresh and sweeter
- so that I have longer with my family
- so that my clothes are more comfortable
- so there is money in the bank
- so I can catch a spider without screaming like a little girl

This reason has to be personal. The reason for Change always comes from an observation, either by you or another. Perhaps you are fed up of being told you smell like an ashtray or are fed up about jokes being made about buttons firing off tight shirts? Maybe you've seen your bank balance and considered not eating this week, or the neighbours have ended up calling the police after you have discovered a spider in the sink? It has to hit a nerve.

Start date

Get a diary out and make an entry in it today. Start the journey as you read this book; delaying it will allow the Mammoth to wriggle past and back to its comfortable rut. Now the basics are done, we need to research how the Change can happen.

Finding out some simple facts about what the change can mean will start to add some emotional weight to it.

Things that can be considered are:

- What are the risks for someone who is obese?
- What does alcohol do to the body?
- Which foods will improve skin conditions?
- What support groups are out there?
- What would my family think if they knew I gambled?
- What are the risks to others from second-hand smoke?
- What do earthworms actually do?

The Mammoth will start to get interested, as this information is starting to show some important facts that are now emotionally worthwhile. It is seeing the plan come together, and this is where we can start to map it all out. The Mammoth will also realise that the Herder is no longer shoving it around to do anything, and this fresh approach gives the Mammoth confidence.

It really does not matter what the Change is about, the principles are all the same.

Whether it is a new job, getting fitter, stopping smoking, losing weight or making more time for your family, if you plan for Change, Change will happen.

Now that the plan is drawn, our Herder needs to team up with the Mammoth to put more detail into the plan and start the map. The map will be a set of instructions that if followed, will guarantee a Change.

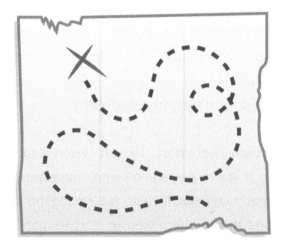

As with any map, we start at the beginning. We plot a course on how we are going to reach the end, and we are going to mark any foreseen traps. Having a diary will keep us on track. Most smartphones have a calendar app that allows us to set reminders, plus we never go anywhere without our phone, unless that is the Change you want to enforce?

The journey is going to be long and, at times, tough, but we have to get both the Herder and the Mammoth to walk the new path.

Our Herder and Mammoth must keep to the path; putting dates, times and locations of where we need to be marks a clear route on the map to Change. The Herder will be up to date of when the next turn will be, and at each turn we can set milestones. We will go into more detail about these in Chapter 17.

The Mammoth needs to be constantly reminded that there is a route and there is a planned journey. Showing the Mammoth this level of detail will allow it to prepare itself and not get frightened. Knowledge and planning shows the Mammoth that there are going to be no surprises, and it will relax more.

Due to being lazy, the Mammoth will forget things and will need a reminder on the calendar. The Mammoth, knowing where it is starting from and knowing where the destination ends, will start to follow the new path, and will be happy to follow it, providing the route does not change.

The Herder can get distracted, so they also need to be reminded of the agreed route and not allowed to wander off. The route needs to be planned for out for the next five to six months in the diary.

It helps that both the Herder and the Mammoth understand that Change is going to take time and not be an overnight exercise. If the diary does not have enough detail, the Mammoth cannot plans its day. Writing times and locations into the diary helps focus the Mammoth's motivation. The more detail about the plan, the better chance of the Mammoth making it a reality.

Changing times, days or activities will give the Mammoth wriggle room, and it will slip out of it. Stick to the plan, and do not make excuses.

Keeping to the agreed path will get easier, as each successfully attended diary appointment will motivate and inspire the Herder and the Mammoth to carry on.

Each completed appointment is a step closer to the final destination and the desired outcome. The path to Change is beginning to become a habit, and the Mammoth likes 'habits'.

Working a normal Monday to Friday nine-to-five job is an easy routine. Plans are easy to put in place and the Mammoth loves routine. The more often a routine can be followed, the better chance we have of it turning into a habit and completing the change.

Shift workers will find any change harder, but it is not impossible, as Change can still happen. It means being a little more organised, putting some extra effort into planning the diary.

If part of the new path is visiting a gym, make sure the map has a reward planned into it. The Mammoth is not going to be excited to see a load of weights going up and down for an hour, so motivate it by promising a relaxing swim and a jacuzzi afterwards. Make the Mammoth know what is expected of it and that there is a reward after.

If quitting smoking is part of the route on the map, write the amount of money being saved each day and total it up day by day.

Let the Mammoth see something is happening for giving up something it has long thought of as a habit. Make a note on the map of when there is enough money in the pot to give back something as a reward. Get the Mammoth to look forward to that part of the journey on the map, where you have promised to do something nice that it will enjoy.

Keep hitting at the Mammoth's positive emotions. Our Herder needs to keep leading the Mammoth down the new path, motivating it on towards the new destination. They have to stick to the plan and keep talking to the Mammoth, making sure that the Mammoth feels comfortable.

Change is not about hitting goals; this is what the Herder enjoys. Reaching a goal is part of the journey, but it has to be fun as well for the sake of the Mammoth.

Without going into detail, there was an interesting research project that took place in 1971, called the Stanford Prison Experiment. A number of students were monitored in a fake prison; half were inmates and the others were prison guards. The outcome was that people fall into a role that society creates for them. It is nature verses nurture all over again.

If you believe that you are always going to be fat, a smoker or scared of ladders, then the Mammoth may need some additional help. Mammoths are herd animals. If it has always been fat, there is chance that it will not want to lose weight by itself.

If, however, it sees a group of other fat Mammoths following a map, each going down a new path heading roughly in the same direction, it will want to join them.

Use support groups, join a diet club, join a job search group, sign up to a dating site, join in timetabled group exercises in the gym, and make a pact with other people to quit doing the very thing you want to stop and do it together. Give the Mammoth the support it needs. Show it that it is not the only one to face these challenges; show it the other Mammoths who face the same journey.

Change can be easier on our Mammoth when others join the cause for change. Our Mammoth will want to be part of a herd and will be more willing to go in the direction of the pack.

Make sure the Herder does not pick the group. They will friend Mo Farah and ask to go running with him at the beginning of the journey, and this will scare the Mammoth. Pick the herd carefully. If the Mammoth cannot keep up and gets left behind, they will return to the comfortable rut before you can do anything about it.

15. PICTURE IT

Focus the Mammoth on the destination.

The Herder can jump on and off the path, and their focus remains on staying the distance. However, there is something that can be done to stop the Mammoth from losing focus. Keeping the lazy Mammoth's attention and motivating it to walk the entire route is a difficult task.

Mammoths do not like the idea of doing something long term, unless there is an emotional gain at the end. It likes quick wins and old habits. The Herder has to help the Mammoth along the path and take its mind off quitting. The Mammoth will, over time, slowly allow the Change to become a habit.

The route has been clearly laid out and the Mammoth is now comfortable with the idea that some effort will mean a positive change. The Mammoth needs motivation to start walking the path, and a reminder to make it across the finishing line.

To do this, we are going to use a picture, a mental image, that can be used time and time again to remind the Mammoth of why Change is needed, and why it is a good idea to keep going.

The image is going to be such a strong pull, that any thought by the Mammoth of giving up is forgotten.

We are going to take time doing this and make sure that we get it right. If we do it properly at the beginning, we run little risk of losing the Mammoth.

Our Herder will also benefit from us doing this at the beginning, as we are giving it a tool to use whenever they feel that they need to motivate the Mammoth and push on. We have to draw such a detailed picture, that we are able to make it seem like a reality. We are going to use every colour imaginable, including every sense we have, and every smell we can link to it.

We have our final destination already marked out from our plan, us being slimmer, fitter, having more money, being happier, or holding a snake. Now we are going to make a picture in our minds of how we are going to look when we complete this change. We are going to see ourselves as having that beach body, ripped muscles, a big white smile, or that look on our face when we see a healthy bank balance. To do this, we are going to have to find something we can carry with us everywhere; a stone, a button, anything that will stay with us when we are awake.

257

Holding the Caveman item in our hand, we are going to use our imagination. Close your eyes if you must, but not just yet; finish reading the instructions first.

With your eyes closed, picture yourself; see your face, your hair, and know it is you. See the detail. If you have hair, see how it sits on you head, even the grey hair you might have. Make it you. Now imagine the biggest and happiest smile on your face, not a grin or a camera smile, but a big fat smile of success and of being happy. Feel the smile spread across your face and note how that feels. Give it a moment and then look at the eyes; they are happy, shiny and relaxed. Feel it for a moment and then move on to your body. See that it is you; your body with your hands, arms, legs and toes. Feel the Caveman stone in your hand.

Now notice that your body feels different. It is taller as if you are tall and proud of your accomplishment. See in your mind's eye that you look different. You look better, better than you have ever looked before, and now let it sink in for a moment. Feel the Caveman stone in your hand.

Take hold of the picture. Add as much detail as you can. Place yourself in a well-known happy place. Make sure that the surrounding images are bright; the picture of the location is making you feel warm, safe and very happy.

Feel the weight of the Caveman stone in your hand.

Next, we add the Change; with us feeling on top of the world, we add the Change. Imagine the fat belly gone, the urge for alcohol disappeared, the feeling of walking past a fruit machine without needing to put our few coins in it, or being up high and holding the top rung of a ladder. Hold the thought for as long as you can; get comfortable with the Change. Feel the weight of the Caveman stone in your hand.

Then look back at your face; see it still smiling, feeling calm. The smile is still there. You are happy without a care in the world. You are still stood in your safe place, feeling all your senses, smelling, touching and watching how your body is reacting. It is strong, holding itself up as a trophy for us to take home. Imagine your body has completed the Change, whether you are finishing a race with a personal best time on the clock, the reduced stomach, or even the hard abs under your shirt. See how your clothes fit, the large arms showing through the shirt. Feel the extra weight of money in your pocket. Take a large breath and feel your clean lungs expand, and sense that feeling of absolute achievement. Feel proud, feel good, and feel the Caveman stone in your hand.

When you have this full picture in your mind, making sure that as much detail has been added, hold the image for as long as you can, then take a 'snapshot' of the changed you. It is not just going to be an image; add the feelings, the colours, the senses. Squeeze your Caveman chosen item, the Caveman stone, or the Caveman button, in your hand, and add your image to the action of squeezing.

When you are done, open your eyes and look at your Caveman stone. Every time you hold the stone, close your eyes and give it a squeeze. See that same image and feel all those senses again; link your stone to your picture. Keep your Caveman stone or button close to hand and in a safe place.

The Caveman stone is there to help you, and should it be lost, forgotten or misplaced, then any replacement item will work just as well. Try and find something of similar size, and feel and keep squeezing it.

We now need to train the Herder. Our Caveman stone has been tuned and ready to use, and we are going to trust the Herder to keep our snapshot image safely rolled up, neatly and to hand. When the Mammoth starts to lose interest in the new path, wanting to eat a doughnut or light up a cigarette, or put some money in a fruit machine, we are going to give the stone a squeeze. This is the signal to the Herder to use the image.

The Herder is going to unroll the image and hold it right in front of the Mammoth, making the Mammoth realise that all those emotions linked to that image is a good thing and it wants to feel them.

The Herder is going to get the Mammoth to remember those feelings and that sense of achievement by showing it the image. The image is going to get the Mammoth to start drooling over the end result and make it want the change.

The snapshot image will be linked to squeezing the Caveman stone, and will keep hitting the Mammoth in its emotional gut. Making it think about how more comfortable it will be, or not worrying about walking up a flight of stairs without stopping to catch its breath, what it is going to spend all that extra cash on. The image will help the Mammoth remember its promise to reach that destination, and it will stick to the path.

Whatever the picture you have made, make it so strong that it is going to grab the Mammoth's attention. Stay away from the negative thoughts. Do not try and cheat by painting a picture of a bowl of salad and then make it taste like a juicy steak, as that will not work. It has to be realistic and it has to motivate the Mammoth by using its emotions.

Mental images and the use of the Caveman stone is great. However, sometimes we can forget to use them. To help conquer Change, we can place some strategically located printed images in those 'danger' places.

'Chuff' charts of our predicted weight loss or that photo of us on our last holiday when we were on the beach, the one with our stomach bulging taped to the fridge door, or that classy picture of us having a cigarette hanging out of our mouths, placed near to the back door where we pop out to have a quick smoke; anything that represents the Change we want or need to make will help remind us of the promise to get to our final destination.

Should you struggle when you are making your snapshot picture, a great way to help create that mental, physical picture is to ask the 'miracle' question;

"Imagine that in the middle of the night, while you were sleeping, a miracle happened and all your troubles you want to change were resolved. When you wake up in the morning, how will you know something had changed, and how would you feel about it?"

There is a very old story of a blind man sat outside on the busy pathway, with an empty tin and a sign. He was collecting money for charity. He had a white stick in his hand and had a written sign saying, "Blind, please help," but everyone walked past and ignored the man.

A young man was sat across the street drinking coffee, watching the blind man and all the people who walked right past him. The young man found a piece of cardboard and wrote a new message on it. He got up, crossed the road and propped the new sign over the blind man's original sign. He dropped some money in the tin and walked away.

As soon as the young man had done this, other people started to put money in the blind man's tin until it was overflowing and people started to place money in the blind man's hand.

The blind man was so overcome with emotion, he said to one of his donators that he had never had such a kind response from people. The donator said that it was his sign that made him want to help. The blind man said, "What, the sign that reads 'Blind, please help'?" and the donator said, "No, the handwritten one that reads, 'It's a beautiful day. You can see it, I cannot.'"

We need to change our thoughts from being problem focused "trousers are too tight" to a solution focus "trousers will fit much better if I lost a little weight."

If we want Change to happen, we should only be making positive images. Focusing on the positives when change needs to happen, we are always happier when a positive thought occurs, and this will motivate and focus the Mammoth's emotions.

If the Mammoth can understand the emotion of what, why and how Change is needed, then the new path will begin to form a 'comfortable rut' or a 'habit'. The Mammoth likes habits and, more importantly, when change starts to show positive effects, Mammoths will not want to fail. The image is about making the Mammoth understand that failure means not reaching the destination.

The Caveman stone will be used a lot when a Change starts. Keeping that Mammoth on the new path takes a lot of effort and a lot of squeezes, but then it will become easier. The constant use of the stone will start to slow down, the Herder will not be holding up the image so often, and the Mammoth will be more comfortable.

The use of images is a strong motivational pull. Documenting the Change journey is also a good idea. On the first day of change, take a photo of you. Then every week, take a new photo, putting all the photos in a folder on the computer.

When the Mammoth wants to get back on the old path, get a camera out and show the Mammoth how far it has come. Stick the pictures up around the house if you want to; keep them in sight and keep them as a constant reminder of the journey so far.

16. MANAGING RESISTANCE

Time to tweak the plan.

Resistance to Change is an external challenge most will face. Here's a short story about a scorpion and a frog;

The scorpion wanted to cross a stream and saw a frog sat on the bank. The scorpion approached the frog and asked if the frog could give it a ride across the stream on its back, but the frog declined, saying that if the scorpion was on its back, then it would surely sting the frog.

The scorpion reasoned that if it were to do that, then both of them would perish. The frog thought about it and agreed that the scorpion had a point, so allowed the scorpion on its back as it started to swim across the stream.

Halfway across the steam, the scorpion stung the frog and they both began to drown. The last few words from the frog were, "Why did you break your promise?" The scorpion knew what its fate was to be, and replied, "Because it is in my nature."

This story is about people refusing to change their ways, a resistance to the requested change. People like to sabotage their own dreams, and those of others.

The scorpion was unable to change its nature and convinced another that it had, but the result was unfortunate for both of them.

A lack of support from others is something known as 'blag'. Telling a friend in a social group that we want to lose weight or to get fitter never happens. Imagine trying to tell someone down the pub that we want to be better people by bringing in a Change. We know most of our friends are going to be laughing in our faces, making us feel inadequate, and even stupid for thinking that Change is a good idea. We will then be forced to buy everyone another round of drinks.

We know how most of our friends are going to react, but if we want them to support us and even join us, there are a few tips we can use. If they have become a large part of our tribe and we want to remain friends with them, then we use their personality trait to our advantage.

If our friend is a Hunter, they will never turn down a challenge and a chance to compete. Use that competitiveness edge to make them want to join in the challenge. Just remember, if you want to cross the finishing line together, you may want to give them some praise on how well they are doing.

If it is a Protector, ask them to help organise the final destination. Make them the planner and get them to organise the group's diary. Give them responsibility and clearly define the finishing line with them. This is all that's needed to get them to want to walk the new path with you.

Gatherers are a little more unsocial and it is hard to get them to buy into any group effort, but if you really want them to join, ask them to do the research and tell them you want to do it their way. Make them the authoritative figure, and asking them to research the best training, route or food should be enough to get them interested enough to join in.

Being open with a Healer is the best way to get them to accept the change. Telling a Healer the personal secret of why we need to make the change, giving them the opportunity to care about us, will perk their interest, and they will want to help. Making it more personal with feelings about why we want to lose weight, stop smoking or any other reason pleading for their help, should be enough. They will feel obliged to watch over you, and even mentor you. They are also the people we should be confiding in when we have slipped or fallen off the wagon. They will be the ones who can motivate us to get back up and keep going.

If those last few paragraphs are a little too far-fetched with the fact that we know our friends and they are not going to support us, then there is another option.

If we are determined to make Changes and our friends are a barrier to that Change, sometimes we have to make a choice. Change needs sacrifice and dedication; if our friends won't change, we can change our friends. If they are not willing to support any Change, they will use opportunities to drag us down each time we meet. We need to consider if they truly are our friend. We should rely on their support, and if not, then it's time for another Change.

If we keep meeting resistance and nothing that we do helps, then we need to have another look at our plan; we may have missed something. Did we look at our environment? Stopping smoking will be easier if we stop hanging around the smoking areas. If we always buy our cigarettes from the same shop or petrol station, then find a new shop or petrol station to use.

If we always buy fast food, a burger from the drive-through that we pass on our way home from work, changing our route home will help take this enticement away. Think about all those habits the Mammoth enjoys and what we can do to keep the Mammoth away from them. Remember, our Mammoth wants us to keep doing the same thing. It likes to stay in its own comfort zone and wants us to do the same. Use the Caveman stone and let the Herder show it the image; get it comfortable with the reasons why Change is needed.

If you try to ignore the Mammoth's constant whining, you will find it is an energy-sapping exercise. Never underestimate how much strength the Mammoth has, and how much power it can have over us.

Resistance can be a real worry for any participant of the Caveman Change Principles. It will always be the Mammoth that gives up, so check to make sure it is not the people around us. If it's not them, check if it is the environment. If it's not our surroundings, then check if there was any poor nurturing or unwilling training being imposed on us. Some resistance issues may need to be explored further and may be beyond the scope of this book, but the principle is the same; check to see why the Mammoth does not want to move forward.

17. CELEBRATE THE MILESTONES

Make the journey enjoyable.

We now have our ultimate final destination, but the journey is going to be a long and unappetising one if we take it all in one go. We have the final Change firmly planted in our minds, and now we have to plan for small targets. These small targets lead to small victories. Each small victory takes us another mile towards our desired larger achievement, the completed Change.

After we have convinced the Mammoth to leave the comfortable rut or its comfort zone, we expect it to try something that it has never achieved before. Our Herder and the Mammoth have teamed up and have shaped the path. Their destination is set and we are all aware that we should not scare the Mammoth. We have an image to hand and the Herder has been taught to show it with a squeeze of the caveman stone, but how can we keep the Mammoth focused and motivated?

A new path is a daunting place for any Mammoth to look down. It does not like being uncomfortable, so we need to make sure the journey is interesting and enjoyable. Mammoths can get bored, and if we focus on the ultimate, end destination, it will not be a quick journey. Changing a Mammoth's habit after years of the same routine is difficult, so we entice it down the path offering treats and emotional rewards as we go, at prearranged milestones along the new path.

Imagine having to drive a car from one end of the country to the other, a distance of 847 miles. How many cars could travel that distance without the need to stop and refuel? Not many, I am guessing. How many drivers would want to drive that entire distance without stopping for a break? Again, not many.

This scenario is the same as our Change journey. Imagine the vehicle being the Mammoth and the driver is the Herder. If we have the right conditions, the right vehicle and the correct rest beforehand, then there is a possibility we could drive that entire distance in one go, but I guarantee without a few stops along the way, the journey will not be enjoyable and things will get very uncomfortable towards the end.

Mammoths like quick wins, not long-term missions. Milestones give the Mammoth a little break and something to focus on. It gives them their quick win, but keeps them in the game for the long haul. Having breaks in the journey does mean setting milestone markers as we head towards the final destination.

Milestones can be made up to mark any small achievement. The final destination might be to have big, strong arms like Arnie Schwarzenegger. The route set that once we are able to lift 250 kg at the gym, we will have enough strength and the 'big guns', and would have completed our Change. That is a long time to spend in the gym to get to our desired change, especially when the first time we go there, we can only lift 20 kg.

Our Herder will be wanting to put 250 kg on a bar and see if they can do it straight away, but in them doing this, it will scare the Mammoth, showing that the task is impossible and the Mammoth will lose faith, wanting to get back into its comfortable rut, as it will be thinking, "What is the point in trying?"

We need to make sure that we do not jump along the path too quickly, that we take each step with care and purpose. Along the path, we will hit milestones that can give instant gratification to the Mammoth. There is no harm in gently pushing the Mammoth along, stating what we want to achieve by the end of this week, but if we are not successful, then we can modify our short-term Change, refocus and try again, but never forgetting what the final destination looks like.

When we set the milestones and we reach them, we have to get our Herder to celebrate it with the Mammoth by doing something that the Mammoth would enjoy doing. If we have given up smoking for a month, celebrate it not by having a smoke, but doing something of value and fun. Go out for a meal with friends or family, or buy yourself a small gift. Whatever you do, make sure the milestone is celebrated.

Putting completed events in our diary, on Facebook, Twitter or a blog, makes the journey a live, living document. It clearly displays the progress we have made and gives motivation to the Mammoth, showing it how far it has already travelled, and hopefully it can start to see the Change already happening.

Keep all chuff charts updated. If it is weight loss, make sure you cross off each pound lost. If it is to stop smoking, show the number of smoke-free days, or the amount of money saved. If it is a change of job, put each step of completing the change in the boxes and cross them off. Always show the start and the final destination on the chart.

1	2	3	4	5	6
7	8	9	10	11	12
13	14	15	16	17	18
19	20	21	22	23	24
25	26	27	28	29	30

Crossing off each small milestone, from the first to the last, gets the Mammoth to mentally picture the journey and for it to tick off each step.

Making the Mammoth feel the joy and excitement of achieving each and every milestone is motivation for it to reach the next one. Before the Mammoth realises it, the Herder will be leading the Mammoth across the finishing line. The path has taken them straight to the new destination, but the journey has not felt so long as it has been broken up into smaller chunks.

These milestones need to form part of the plan for the journey. Having clearly put milestones in a Change proposal, it acts as a marker for the Mammoth and keeps it focused. It can motivate and encourage it to continue on with the journey to reach the next one.

When the Mammoth is flagging, getting slower and there is fear of it getting spooked off the new path, and the use of the Caveman stone may have been overused, we may need to reassess a milestone. If it is going to be a real struggle to get to the next milestone, we do not want to let the Mammoth give up and quit. We need to re-evaluate the next milestone; would it hurt if we added a new one, a little closer, and celebrate that one instead?

Celebrating any milestone is an uplifting experience for the Mammoth. That extra 10 kg as planned might be a little too much this occasion, so celebrate an extra 5 kg. Choose ones that informs the Mammoth what it has achieved so far to keep our Mammoth interested on a different level. Finding an occasion to celebrate is easy; count how many gym sessions have been completed since the start of the journey, find something to show progress is being made, the amount of stairs you can climb without getting out of breath, how much money you have saved, how much closer we can get to our toes, anything to show an improvement. Find a new motivational milestone; your Mammoth will like the recognition of hitting a new one, and it will be inspired to continue along the journey.

Milestones are great for motivational needs, and they are also useful to be used as a restart marker along the path. Should something spook our Mammoth and it runs off back towards the comfortable rut, all is not lost. Our Herder should chase after the Mammoth and catch it up. Give the Caveman stone a squeeze and let the Herder use the image to get the Mammoth's attention again.

The Mammoth will need a little time to calm itself down, but the use of the stone will help.

Try and get the Herder to catch the Mammoth before it hits the last milestone, and consider that as the new starting point. Pushing the Mammoth back to where they ran off will spook it again. Let it remember what the last milestone felt like and get it to work back up to the next one.

Something spooked the Mammoth, so when starting from the last milestone, take it easy. Get the Herder to watch the Mammoth and walk it steadily through the next milestone. When the Mammoth does pass through the marker, celebrate it like no other. Get the excitement going in the Mammoth and show it that the last milestone was worth all the effort.

Change is not a race, so don't let the Herder push ahead too fast. The end game is to get the Mammoth over the finishing line. Use milestones along the journey and make sure they are celebrated. Little Changes combined makes one big Change in the end.

∾

18. REACH THE DESTINATION.

You have broken the habit.

Change is stressful and, if not managed correctly, will cause a large number of button presses, adding to our already stressful lives. All the work, dedication and planning that needed to be put into Change, then watching it fail because the Mammoth got spooked, will cause stress. Too many people embark on a Change journey and do not realise how much hard work is involved to reach the end destination. To most, it can equate to starting to run a marathon; at the start, it is easy, but the journey gets harder without doing any preparation. If we want to be serious about Change, then we have to do some work before we step off down the new path.

The final destination may be to lose weight, stop smoking, get fitter, to become a better parent by helping your child with their homework, to treat the love of your life with more respect and compassion, or get a better job. Regardless of the Change, the only person who controls it is you. The Caveman Change Principles remain the same for any change that is needed, required or wanted. Following them will help everyone become successful in their Change quest.

Bringing all the Change Principles together, they look a little like this:

- Make a written promise with the Herder and the Mammoth.
- Describe the desired final destination.
- Work out how they are both going to get there by making a plan.
- Map a route to help them both with the first step on the journey.
- Make sure they both understand they have to cross the line together.
- Use a snapshot image of the desired change.
- Use a Caveman stone to remind the Herder to show the image to the Mammoth.
- Manage any resistance by checking the company that you keep is not holding you back.
- Make sure the journey is broken up into shorter chunks; put milestones out as markers.
- Celebrate every passing of a milestone.
- Focus on the destination, and keep the Mammoth from getting spooked.

Wherever the final destination is, make sure that you have set the intent, mapped the path, given it meaning and drawn a picture for the Mammoth, using all of the senses.

Make sure our Herder and the Mammoth set off on the journey together, that they know the direction they are heading, and the Herder is not allowed to go off-track. The Herder has to lead the Mammoth and not resort to pushing it, as the Mammoth has to make its own mind up. Make sure that each milestone is counted and recorded, and both remain together as the finishing line gets closer.

The final destination, the finishing line, is as important to the journey as the path itself. Once the destination has been mapped and planned, motivating the Mammoth is going to be hard. If we try and move the finishing line, the Mammoth will get spooked, lose interest and run back to its comfortable rut.

The Caveman Change Principles needs to be followed and a commitment made. Habits are hard to break and if failing to Change happens, the 'failure' may turn into a habit as well.

A choice needs to be made right at the beginning before the Herder and the Mammoth are going to be asked to walk a new path. We have to fully commit to supporting them if we want any Change to happen. Failure is not an option.

The Caveman Change Principles will only work if all of these stages have been worked out, planned, written down and religiously kept to. It may seem like there is no harm in wanting to make improvements to a plan or making a situation better once the journey has begun, but do not do it. Finish the journey first before any amendments are made.

Once the finishing line has been crossed, celebrate it as planned. Use the money you have saved or bend the credit card a little; make sure it is a proper celebration to show the Mammoth what success looks like. Never extend a path by adding to a plan; make a completely new one once the journey has been complete, and start the process all over again.

Success breeds success. Mammoths like to win and will suddenly have an emotional interest in completing another Change and it will be up for another challenge. Taking a break can teach the Mammoth a new habit, that of taking a break. Strike while the iron is hot, and the Mammoth will continue to work hard.

Keep the Mammoth calm and do not allow a situation to be created where it can get spooked. Stick to the plan and this removes the fear of failure.

Using all the tricks you have been shown in this book, images, Caveman stones, chuff charts, anything at all that will help remind the Mammoth of the reason it wants to change. Put messages up from people who used to make fun about you being big, having a beer belly or not fitting in a chair, or the one where people complain about it stinking of smoke after you've had a cigarette. Put them around your workspace, and keep them as reminders of why our Mammoth does not want to return to the starting line.

Keep reminding the Mammoth how far it has come and keep it going in the right direction. Keep our Herder under control and remind it that they have signed a promise. Train the Herder and use the Caveman stone when needed. Make sure the Herder does not try and take a shortcut where they lose the Mammoth; all the effort will be lost.

The Caveman Change Principles aim is to get the Mammoth and the Herder over that finishing line together. There will always be issues that will come up. There will always be some resistance to manage. Some people will do anything to derail our Herder and the Mammoth's chances because they are fearful of Change themselves.

Stay focused, keep to the plan, use the snapshot image, and one final note from the author; good luck, and never give up.

For useful downloads,
monthly newsletter updates
and worksheets,
please visit the website:

www.carlrosierjones.com
www.cavemanprinciples.co.uk

THE CAVEMAN PRINCIPLES

Lightning Source UK Ltd.
Milton Keynes UK
UKHW02f0141030318
318822UK00007B/91/P